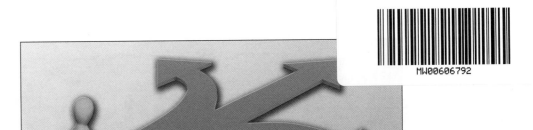

Helping Young People Learn
Self-Regulation

*Lessons, Activities & Worksheets
for Teaching the Essentials of
Responsible Decision-Making & Self-Control*

A RESOURCE FOR WORKING WITH INDIVIDUALS, SMALL GROUPS AND CLASSROOMS (GRADES K–8)

by
Brad Chapin, M.S., LCP, LMLP
Matthew Penner, M.S.W., LMSW

youth light
inc.

© 2013, 2012 by YouthLight, Inc.
Chapin, SC 29036

Cover Design and Layout by Diane Florence
Project Editing by Susan Bowman

ISBN: 9781598501124

Library of Congress Number
2011942395

10 9 8 7 6 5 4 3
Printed in the United States

Dedication

The authors would like to dedicate this book to all of the children and adults who are struggling through life without ever being taught how to regulate themselves. This book was written in an effort to reach those individuals and provide a sense of hope that things can be better.

Acknowledgements

We would like to thank our families for their love and support through our continued effort to educate others. We would also like to thank those mentors along the way who have inspired us to help those in need.

Table of Contents

Table of Contents

Section 5: Anger Management and Small Group Core Curricula

Introduction

Why Self-regulation?

As a professional in these fast-paced times, one is constantly faced with the challenges of demonstrating outcomes, operating on a tight budget, working long hours, and serving a population that often seems more intense and challenging every day. With all of these pressures, it is easy to become overwhelmed. The authors of this book are very sensitive to these constraints, and have put a great deal of thought into providing readers with strategies that are cost and time efficient.

We also understand that it can be very challenging to sift through the numerous research articles, books, and approaches developed during the past several decades. Over the years, we have filtered through that information to find the common themes and patterns in those approaches that are effective. The driving force behind this strategy guide is this question.

"If you had only 5 or 10 minutes to spend with a child, what is the most important skill you would teach?"

With so many children struggling in so many areas, how could there be one answer to this question? After working with hundreds of families, reading countless books and articles, conducting research, and speaking with parents and professionals around the country, the answer has become clear. We found ourselves returning to the same core strategies that made sense to us and the people we worked with. They are practical and they work! The common theme we found accurately described the negative issues we were seeing, and it also embodied the positive aspects that we wanted to help children develop. It was summed up in one term.....Self-regulation.

The term Self-regulation is no longer reserved for solely impulse-control issues. Self-regulation is a broad term that encompasses most of the major issues we see people struggling with. At first, this seemed to be way too obvious and simple. So we, as many people do these days, tried to complicate it by adding other concepts, terms and domains. But we kept ending up in the same place. Still not satisfied, we attempted to find issues that had nothing to do with Self-regulation. This also proved to be a difficult task, but we ask that you feel free to try it for yourself. When looking for a philosophy or framework to operate from, this is an important step. One must feel comfortable with his/her approach, but not so comfortable that he/she is unable or unwilling to challenge it.

Introduction

In the literature, Self-regulation, or this concept of regulating one's physical, emotional and behavioral responses, has been closely associated with several other terms including emotional regulation, self-control, and coping (Macklem, 2008). In the spirit of presenting simple, practical and useful information, the philosophy and strategies contained in this book are based on a broad and flexible definition of Self-regulation.

Based on our interpretation of the literature and our experience in the field, we have come to understand that Self-regulation is a universal skill that is directly related to success in every major area of functioning. In fact, Shonkoff & Phillips (2000) refer to Self-regulation as a cornerstone of childhood development that cuts across all domains of behavior. It predicts academic success better than IQ (Duckworth & Seligman, 2005). It also correlates highly with longevity and well-being (Grossarth-Maticek & Eysenck, 1995; Moffitt et al., 2011). In other words, those who regulate themselves well have higher academic performance, are more successful and live longer, happier lives than those who do not.

 This is a short list of additional topics that we believe are related to Self-regulation:

Academic Performance	Cognitive Flexibility	Locus of Control	Self-efficacy
Aggression/Violence	Depression	Happiness	Self-esteem
Anger	Emotional Control	Oppositional Defiance	Social interaction
Anxiety	Executive Function	Mood Regulation	Success
Attention	Impulse Control	Motivation	Trauma
Attribution	Learned Helplessness	School Safety	Well-being

This list is not complete, but it should help you determine whether or not this book is for you. If you are a parent or your profession involves helping children or adults with any of these topics, you will find this information to be useful, practical and effective.

What are the strategies based on?

In an effort to save time, we will use a simple diagram of the philosophy and condense a great deal of the information supporting this program down into eight Assumptions. Approaching serious issues without a framework or philosophy to operate from can be devastating. You can feel confused and overwhelmed. Your attempts to help will not only seem scattered and confusing to you, but also to the child. The chances of success will diminish significantly. This diagram illustrates the fundamental framework for the approach.

Diagram of Self-regulation Training Philosophy

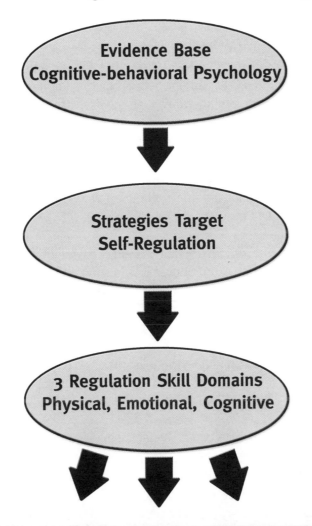

Evidence Base
Cognitive-behavioral Psychology

Strategies Target
Self-Regulation

3 Regulation Skill Domains
Physical, Emotional, Cognitive

Academic Performance	Emotional Control	Motivation
Aggression/Violence	Executive Function	School Safety
Anger	Impulse Control	Self-efficacy
Anxiety	Learned Helplessness	Self-esteem
Attention	Locus of Control	Social interaction
Attribution	Longevity	Success
Cognitive Flexibility	Happiness	Trauma
Depression	Oppositional Defiance	Well-being

Introduction

The following list of eight Assumptions provides the supporting principles for the framework. Many of these assumptions are consistent with cognitive-behavioral psychology. Again, we encourage you to research this information on your own.

Assumption #1 – Children will do well if they can. It is our job as responsible adults to help children navigate and remove barriers in their lives (Greene & Ablon, 2006). We do not believe that we are here to control children. Our goal is for children to grow to manage themselves. We are helpful guides.

Assumption #2 – One must be physically calm to effectively engage in problem-solving, perform well and learn (Yerkes & Dodson, 1908; Goleman, 1998). We know from medical, educational, and psychological studies that higher level brain functions are impaired during times of physical distress. This applies to both adults and children.

Assumption #3 – Human beings have little control over their environment, but a great deal of control over their responses to their environment. Our perception of the event is more powerful, with regards to our emotional and behavioral response, than the event itself (Ellis, 1962). We must first believe that we can have some control over ourselves before we will attempt to change (Kuhl, 1984).

Assumption #4 – The relationship is likely the most important variable when trying to help someone change (Hubble, Duncan & Miller, 1999). This assumption has been replicated for decades in the psychological research literature.

Assumption #5 – Cognitive-behavioral psychology works. Strategies from the realm of cognitive-behavioral psychology have consistently been shown to effectively help individuals change their mood and behavior. There are now several hundred randomized research studies to support this approach (Beck & Fernandez, 1998; Butler, Chapman, Forman & Beck, 2006).

Assumption #6 – Effective Self-regulation is critical for success and happiness. Those individuals who have well-developed self-regulation skills have a better chance for happiness and coping with life's challenges (Baumeister, Heatherton, & Tice, 1994; Duckworth & Seligman, 2005; Masten & Coatsworth, 1998).

Assumption #7 – In order to be effective, we need to meet children where they are currently functioning (Greene & Ablon, 2006; Bailey, 2001). Not matching your strategies to fit the child's current level of skill will result in frustration and failure.

Introduction

Assumption #8 – Do not assume that children have learned anything about how to regulate their own behaviors in a healthy way. Many of the children we work with have not had exposure to positive self-regulatory examples. With the right strategies and information, people can change their thoughts and behaviors. If we don't believe people are capable of change, we are all wasting a great deal of time and energy.

To be consistent with our practical efforts, we did not go into great detail to describe the foundations for these Assumptions. If you have questions about these Assumptions, please feel free to research the information further, or contact the authors of this book.

One last comment about this approach is that we believe the child must be engaged in the process for it to be successful. We gained a great deal of experience with this idea during the creation and implementation of the Challenge Software Program for children. This unique, web-based tool utilizes animated scenarios and games to engage children quickly and teach them the basics of self-control. It can be found at www.cpschallenge.com. In line with the theme of the Challenge Software Program, we have designed the strategies in this book to be engaging and fun.

What are the 3 Areas of Self-regulation?

When regulating one's self, one must have skills for calming the body, skills for expressing emotions appropriately, and skills for moderating thoughts to problem-solve effectively. Therefore, we feel it makes sense to divide Self-regulation into 3 Functional Categories.

3 Functional Categories of Self-regulation

1. **Physical**
2. **Emotional**
3. **Cognitive**

The following few paragraphs offer a short description of the relevance for these 3 functional domains.

Introduction

Physical

First, we must revisit Assumption #2. This assumption indicates that we cannot engage in any of our other interventions until the child is calm. Therefore, teaching the physical strategies that focus on calming should be a priority and come first.

At the most basic level, the physical component of Self-regulation consists of moderating the Fight/Flight stress response in the lower regions of the brain, or Brain Stem. When the stress response in the Brain Stem is activated, chemical reactions take place in the body that cause adrenaline and cortisol to be released. Additionally, the heart rate and blood-flow to the major muscle groups increase in an effort to prepare the body to fight or run (Cannon, 1932). The capacity for activity in the Higher portions of the brain, required for effective problem-solving, is decreased. Therefore, it's critical that we de-activate this Stress response before we move forward with Higher level interventions.

Physical strategies include:
- Repetitive movement involving the major muscle groups
  (Ex. - bouncing a ball)
- Regulation of breathing (Ex. – deep breathing exercises)
- Redirection or distraction (Ex. – leaving the stressful situation)
- Bilateral Stimulation of the brain – activities that engage both sides of the brain (Ex. - Crossing and uncrossing your arms or legs)

The importance of developing physical calming skills for good Self-regulation cannot be over-stated. In line with Assumption #7, almost all problem-situations involve some degree of Brain Stem activation and the need to implement physical strategies first in order to move forward. As with most skills, development of adequate physical calming skills requires practice when the child is in a non-stressed state. In Chapter 2, we will provide you with several ideas for addressing physical regulation.

Emotional

As stated in Assumption #6, effective regulation is crucial for emotional well-being. One of the major goals of improving emotional regulation is teaching the child about his/her ability to control his/her own emotional responses to events. But before addressing this concept with children, some basic skills need to be in place. First, the child needs to have some language to label their emotions accurately. When a child is experiencing an intense emotion, one of the first things we want them to do is to communicate that feeling using words. This not only indicates to others what the child is feeling, but also engages higher functioning areas of the brain and can start the calming process. We often hear professionals asking children to "use their words." Before they can do this effectively, there needs to be some practice of this skill.

Secondly, children need to be able to describe the intensity of the emotions they are feeling. Rating of the intensity provides more information that helps the child and the adult decide what needs to happen next with regard to intervention. For example, if a child rates his anger at a 9 on a scale of 1 to 10, your intervention would be much different than if the rating was a 2. This rating system is also a good way to show progress during the calming process. It can let you and the child know when he/she is ready to re-engage with peers, or in the learning process.

The third part of emotional regulation requires the ability to express emotions in healthy ways. This typically includes the utilization of physical calming skills to moderate the feeling that is being expressed. Being able to correctly identify the feeling, rate the intensity, and moderate the expression of emotions constitute healthy emotional regulation.

In Chapter 3 we will provide strategies that you can use to help children become better at identifying, rating and expressing their emotions. We will also address what may be the most empowering skill a child can learn with regards to Self-regulation. This is the understanding that we control our own emotional/behavioral responses; we are not controlled by others. This higher level of intervention encompasses more executive functions including planning, organization, and thinking about their own thought processes. This leads us to the importance of understanding the connections between thoughts, emotions and actions which is necessary for the development of a more pro-active belief system. Challenging a belief system like this leads us into the realm of Cognitive strategies.

Handwritten margin notes: verbalize feelings / rate intensity / express / (brain development)

Introduction

Cognitive

Equally as important as the physical and emotional domains of self-regulation, is the development of cognitive regulation skills. This higher skill level involves more critical thinking, self-monitoring, and the development of insight. Within this domain we are developing the abilities to modify thoughts, plan responses, process events, problem-solve and prevent problems.

To illustrate the importance of the cognitive aspect of self-regulation, let's look at a common example that children often struggle with. That is the belief that others "make" them feel a certain way. This reactive belief system allows the child to take no responsibility for their own emotions and actions, creating a barrier for positive change. Children, and unfortunately many adults, spend way too much time and energy trying to change external things, rather than focusing their efforts on their own internal processes where they have a great deal more control.

Drawing on Assumption #3, this task of convincing children to focus on what they can control is crucial for success. If you don't address this issue early, your other interventions may not be successful because the child will not "believe" he/she can do anything about the issue. This is also a very empowering lesson for a child to learn. He/she will learn that other people and events don't dictate his/her feelings and behaviors. They will also realize that they have been allowing other people and events to "control" them. This shift in thinking is very important in order to move forward.

Introduction

How do I use this book?

In line with our practical philosophy, we have intentionally designed this approach to be applied in a flexible manner and implemented in many different settings. The strategies can be used individually or with small groups. The skills are universal and necessary for success. Therefore, the strategies can be useful for all children, including high risk and identified populations. Additionally, these strategies lend themselves to being used one-at-a-time for specific issues, or as an organized set of lessons to maximize self-regulation and skill development.

The diagram of the supporting philosophy (p. 7) illustrates the simple and practical flow of this approach. It is based soundly in cognitive-behavioral psychology and targets the 3 areas of Self-regulation: physical, emotional, and cognitive. We recommend that children move progressively through the functional domains by first developing the Physical skills, then Emotional skills, and finally the Cognitive skills. As the diagram indicates, there are several problem areas that you can target with this approach.

As with any approach, the first step is a good assessment. When working individually with a child, complete a brief assessment using the child's background information and the provided Assessment Tool (p. 16) to identify strengths and needs regarding physical, emotional, and cognitive regulation skills. This will provide you with direction on which type of strategies you will need to focus on first.

Most children will start with physical strategy development, then move to the emotional, and lastly to the cognitive skills. Please remember to consider the developmental and ability levels when setting goals for skill development. Children who are too young, or have cognitive impairments may not be ready for the Cognitive strategies. However, even very young children can learn to master the Physical and Emotional strategies.

Once you have identified the problem area(s), use the Problem/Strategy Matrix Tool (p. 14) to help you find strategies that specifically match the problem area(s) you want to target. As you can see in this matrix, several problem areas are listed across the top. Once you've found the problem area you are wanting to target, look below it to see which strategies are designed to address the area Specifically (S) or are Related (R) to the problem area.

Introduction

Problem/Strategy Matrix

	Strategies	Anger & Aggression	Anxiety & Worry	Self-esteem & Sadness	Social Interaction & Bullying	Oppositional & Impulse Control	Page no.
P H Y S I C A L	Cooling the Flame	S	R		R	S	19
	Melting Freeze	S	S		R	S	23
	Warning Signs	S	S	S	R	S	25
	Take a Hike	S	S	R	S	S	28
	A Safe Place	R	S	R	S		31
	Animal Stretches	S	S			R	34
E M O T I O N A L	You Can't Make Me Laugh	S		S	S	R	37
	Feelings Clip Art	S	S	S			40
	The Emotional Safe	S	S	S			43
	Emotional Rain Gauge	S	S	R			46
	Emotional Knots	S	S	S	S	R	49
	Emotional Overflow	S	R		R	R	51
	Free Emotional Expression	S	S	S	S	S	53
C O G N I T I V E	Don't Take the Bait	S		R	S	S	57
	Defiance Trap	S				S	60
	Finish Your Thoughts	S	S	S			63
	The Domino Effect	S	S	S	S	S	68
	Magnetic Thoughts	R	S	S		R	71
	Detection Radar	R	S		S		74
	Shaping Your Thoughts	R	S	S			76
	Problem Solving Remote	R	R	R	S	S	81
	Grow a Thought		S	S	R		84
	Target Practice	S	S	S	R		87

S = Specifically designed to target problem area

R = Related and useful for problem area

Introduction

The following example illustrates how the Assessment/Progress Monitoring Tool guides the process from the beginning stages of assessment through the implementation of specific strategies and the progress monitoring. As you can see from the example, this simple tool provides a concise summary of the issues addressed, the strategies used to target the issues, and the child's progress toward the development of self-regulation skills within each of the skill domains.

Example:

Johnny is a 10-year-old boy who is often disruptive in class. He has frequent anger outbursts. Once he becomes angry, he stays agitated for over an hour and continues to struggle when he returns to class. These outbursts can be triggered by other students or by the teacher. He seems to believe that "things have to be a certain way or else" and it is obvious that he does not believe he has control over his actions. He believes that others "make" him angry and can be openly defiant. His grades and cognitive abilities are average for his age. He comes from a single-parent home. These behaviors are also being reported at home.

Introduction

Johnny's Assessment/Progress Monitoring Tool over an 8-week period:

	Behaviors To Address	1st Rating (1-10)	Strategy Used (See Matrix)	Response	Outcome Rating (1-10)
PHYSICAL					
Recognizes physical signs	Explosive outbursts, poor recognition	1	My Warning Signs	Completed first week, continue to practice	8
Uses healthy calming strategies successfully	Stays escalated for extended periods, Needs development	1	Cooling the Flame, Melting Freeze	Mastered after 3 weeks, Calms down much quicker	7
EMOTIONAL					
Identifies feelings	Only Anger, Needs development	1	Emotional Knots	Much better at labeling	8
Recognizes responsibility and ability to change	Blames others	1	You Can't Make Me Laugh	Enjoyed activity, still working at this concept	6
Expresses Emotions in healthy ways	Yells, throws things, hits others Needs development	1	Free Healthy Expression	Will process when calm, not yelling or hitting	7
COGNITIVE					
Replaces Unhealthy thoughts with healthy beliefs	Confused, thinks others are against him Needs development	1	Finish Your Thoughts	Beginning to understand impact of thoughts on emotions/behaviors	5
Uses Cognitive strategies to problem-solve	Needs development	1	Defiance Trap	Processes well after, working on predicting ahead of time	5

STRENGTHS:	BARRIERS:
Likes music, smart, has friends, good at sports	Rigid thinking, anger has built up, difficult to build rapport with

Introduction

In addition to using the strategies to build your own tailored curriculum based on the individual needs of each child, the final chapter of this book contains two different examples of an eight-session curriculum. The first example illustrates how the book can be used with an individual child who is struggling with Anger issues. The second is a Small Group curriculum designed to provide the core skills necessary for healthy self-regulation.

Goals and Expectations

Our goal with this book is to provide you with practical, effective and engaging strategies that can be easily implemented to address a wide variety of common issues to help children succeed. Ideally, we believe that teaching and learning Self-regulation involves more than just working through a set of interventions. We see it as a philosophy for approaching and coping with the challenges of life. Self-regulation involves learning and implementing a skill set that is crucial for success and overall well-being.

Using this approach also allows you to incorporate many of the techniques you already use with children. We believe if you were to review your favorite techniques, you would find that they will fit into this model within the categories of Physical, Emotional or Cognitive strategies. We encourage you to use this framework to help organize your approach and incorporate your favorite strategies, your interests and your unique specialties to make it your own. The practical layout of this approach allows you to easily create a curriculum that is tailor-made for each child, or group, that you work with.

It is evident that we will never have the time, energy or resources to specifically train children how to respond to each of the thousands of difficult situations they will encounter in a lifetime one by one. We will not be able to identify every single trigger (antecedent) that could potentially throw a child off course, or follow them around to be sure we provide the appropriate consequence for each of their behaviors. We will never be able to make life go perfectly, or control how others treat them. It's also very unlikely that we will be able to identify and successfully challenge each of the unhealthy thoughts they have. Given our limitations, it makes sense that we provide them with the effective "tools" necessary to cope with these situations on their own. Helping children develop Self-regulatory skills will provide them with the ability to make healthy choices about their thoughts, feelings and behaviors on their own in most situations. That is our wish for each child and the purpose of this approach.

Physical Strategies

As we mentioned in Section 1, there is a logical reason for starting with the physical regulation skills. In order to be able to discuss emotions and engage in problem-solving we must be physically calm. Children who haven't developed this skill are still regularly operating in a fight/flight/shut-down mode that inhibits their ability to progress. When children are in this state, they are not able to learn or benefit from common forms of intervention. They are not open to rational communication or problem-solving and may not respond well to traditional forms of behavior modification.

We cannot overstate the importance of having well-developed physical calming skills. From our experience, even a child with the most serious of issues can function in the home or learning environment if they can physically calm themselves down before they explode. So, before initiating higher level interventions, or expecting children to make progress, be sure they have developed the skills necessary for physical regulation.

The following interventions are designed to teach children the basic skill of physical regulation. These strategies can be used one-at-a-time, or as part of a set curriculum to address a specific problem area. Remember to use the Assessment Tool (p. 16) and the Problem/Strategy Matrix (p. 14) to help you decide which physical strategies to try based on the problem areas you want to address.

→ **Note: The physical strategies are the only strategies that should be implemented when a child is upset.**

Cooling the Flame

Purpose Children who struggle with self-regulation often have difficulty calming down when they become upset. This strategy teaches children who are angry how to take control of their anger by utilizing visualization and deep breathing to harness their emotion and pro-actively "cool" it down. In this activity the child will both Give and Receive visual images that signal the body to calm down.

Materials
• Cooling the Flame Version 1 or Version 2 Worksheet
• Color crayons or markers

Process Note: For best results, familiarize children with this strategy when they are calm.

1. If using this strategy with a child that is currently upset, separate the child from the situation.

2. Provide him/her with the materials and use the following script to guide the child:

→ "Try to color this first circle to match how angry you feel right now. Try to picture all of your anger going into this ball. I will help you this first time."

→ Encourage the child to use the color Red and possibly to draw flames or some other indicators of how angry he/she is.

→ "Now, take a slow, deep breath and let it out. Then I want you to color the next ball that shows how angry you feel now."

→ Encourage the child to draw something that looks less intense, possibly orange and with less flames.

→ "I want you to take another deep breath before we move on, and then we will color another ball."

3. Continue in this fashion until you reach the last ball. The color sequence should move naturally from Red to Orange to Yellow to Green/Blue, with variations in-between.

4. When finished, draw the child's attention to the significant difference between the first ball and the last ball. You might say:

→ "Wow! The last ball looks much more calm than the first one."

Cooling the Flame (continued)

Variations
- Using the Computer – For those children who have an interest in Technology, this variation works well. Create the Circles in the MS Paint™ program. Have the child use the controls in the program to complete the exercise rather than on paper.

- For a child who has mastered this basic version, move to using the Cooling the Flame Version 2 handout to move toward better emotion recognition and self-monitoring in relation to the Calming aspect of the exercise.

- Use the Challenge Software Program found at www.cpschallenge.com for an interactive experience with the Cooling the Flame strategy.

Cooling the Flame

Cooling the Flame

ANNOYED	PRETTY FRUSTRATED	REALLY ANGRY

Physical Strategies

Melting Freeze

Purpose Children who do not regulate well have difficulty calming down physically when they are upset. This strategy was designed to help a child who is upset calm down. It can also be practiced with children who are calm but require regular relaxation or a calming experience periodically to remain calm and prevent escalation. It can also be used prior to, or following, the processing of an upsetting issue to help the child become physically calm.

Materials • Melting Freeze Worksheet

Process 1. If using this strategy with a child that is currently upset, separate the child from the situation.

2. Use the worksheet to illustrate the process and the following script to guide the child:

→ "We are going to pretend that our bodies are like water. When water freezes it gets very hard and turns to ice. When it warms up it melts, drips and turns into a puddle on the floor."

3. You will start with the lower sections of the body and work upward toward the head and neck.

→ For each section say, "Make your _____ muscles tight and hard like ice. Keep them tight and make them freeze while we count to 5."

→ After reaching 5 say, "Now we are going to melt the ice. Take a deep breath and imagine that your _____ muscles are melting. We are going to count backwards from 5 to 0. When we reach zero our _____ muscles will be like a puddle and they will feel loose and relaxed."

4. Repeat this process for the legs, stomach/back, arms, shoulders/neck and head/face areas of the body.

Variation • Complete this exercise as a group activity at the same time each day to reduce tension and promote a calm atmosphere.

Melting Freeze

"Pretend that your muscles are like water. Now we are going to change the form of our muscles to frozen (tense) like ice and then back to melted (relaxed) like water."

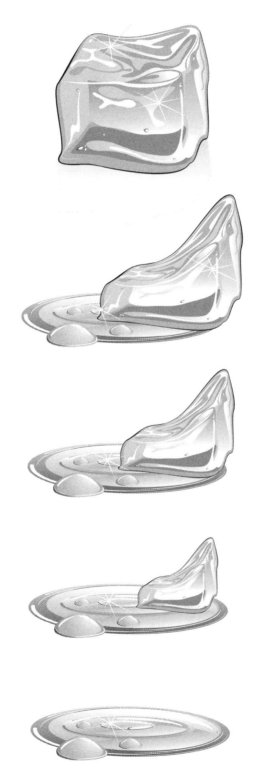

Physical Strategies

Warning Signs

Purpose   One of the first steps in diffusing emotional upset is successful recognition of the physical changes that take place in the body. Although there are common signs, such as fist clenching and stomach upset, each person has their own individual specific signs that are unique.

This exercise is designed to identify and clarify the child's individual physical signs of becoming upset. Upset can mean angry, sad, worried, etc.

Materials   • Warning Signs worksheet, writing utensil

Process   1. Present the child with the hand-out and a writing utensil. Ask him/her to draw a full-body self-portrait in the space provided.

2. As he/she draws, begin to discuss examples of changes that happen physically when people become upset. You can use a story to illustrate this process.

→ For example, you may say, "Last week I was at the store and I was ready to check out. Just then, someone jumped in front of me in the check-out line. I remember feeling my face get hot and my stomach feeling upset. When I noticed these signs, I knew I was getting angry and needed to calm down before I did something I would feel bad about later."

3. As the child completes the drawing ask him/her to connect the signs that he/she has experienced from the list to the specific areas of the body on the drawing. Then ask the child to list any other signs that he/she has experienced that are not on the list in the extra spaces provided.

4. At the bottom of the page, write in a strategy that will work to diffuse signals that the child has identified. For example, counting to 5 and taking a few deep breathes, or one of the other Physical calming strategies in this book.

Warning Signs (continued)

Variations
- Use a computerized drawing program, such as MS Paint™, to create the drawing and then circle or label the areas of the body affected by the individual signs. Be specific and creative. For example, if they describe butterflies in the stomach, add butterflies to the picture and connect them to the stomach.

- Group activity – Use large paper and create life-sized drawings. Label the different areas with the symptoms.

- Select an age-appropriate video clip from Youtube™, or similar website, of a person becoming upset and identify the warning signs witnessed as a group.

My Warning Signs

Common Warning signs

1. Upset stomach

2. Headache

3. Clinched fists

4. Loud voice

5. Red face

6. Restless, fidgety, twitchy

7. Heart beating faster or louder

8. _____

9. _____

10._____

How I Calm down when these changes happen:

_____

_____

_____

_____

_____

_____

_____

Draw Yourself Here

Physical Strategies

Take a Hike

Purpose Children struggling with self-regulation often have difficulty walking away from situations that trigger them to become upset or feel threatened.

This strategy is used to teach children the benefit of "walking away" when they become upset before they say or do something they will regret. This strategy utilizes the analogy of going for a hike. It makes use of distraction, involves repetitive physical movement, and encourages relaxation. It may be particularly useful at the beginning of the school year or other transition times where a child may not be familiar with his/her environment. This strategy can also be part of a safety or crisis plan.

Materials • Take a Hike Worksheet and a writing utensil

Process This two-part strategy should be introduced when the child is calm and put into action when the child appears angry, frustrated, or anxious.

1. Begin this strategy with a short description of a hike. You might say something like:

   → "Today we are going to plan for a hike. Hikes can be relaxing and take our minds off of things that are bothering us. We are going to plan a hike that we can take if we start to feel upset. Before we go, we need to make sure that we know where we are going and that we have what we need."

2. Use the space at the bottom of the handout to create a short, safe route around the room, or area nearby, for the hike.

3. Using the handout, begin to discuss the steps taken to prepare for a hike like stretching. Draw attention to the fact that it's a good idea to stretch and take a few deep breaths before a hike. Demonstrate a few simple stretches.

4. Next, label the map. Use as many of the items listed 1-7 on the handout as needed. Ask the child if there are any others areas or stops he/she would like to label on the map.

Physical Strategies

Take a Hike (continued)

5. Review the Things to remember for a Safe Hike:

→ Take someone with you, or check with someone before you go

→ Do a few stretches before you begin

→ Drink some water on your trip

→ Use safe zones to relax and feel comfortable and safe

→ Mark something on the map that is interesting to look at

6. Say, "Now, we need to test out our Map."

→ Do a walk-through of the hike together. Remember to practice the exercise when the child is calm. This will help improve the likelihood of the child being able to successfully implement the strategy when he/she really needs it.

Variations
- Use a program like MS Paint™ on the computer to construct a map and try it out on the computer before using it in real life.

- Create a "pack" with cards that indicate each individual step of the journey. For example:

→ 1 card that says: Stretch first

→ 3 cards that say: Take a deep breath

→ 1 card that says: Get a drink

→ 1 card that says: Find Safe Zone

Take a Hike

Places to label on your map:

1. Safe Zones

2. Relaxing spots

3. Places to eat or drink

4. People that can help

5. Things to look at along the way

6. _____

7. _____

** Remember to stretch and take some deep breaths before, during and after your hike.

Draw Your Map Here

Physical Strategies

A Safe Place

Purpose One of the most common reasons for reactivity is when one feels threatened. This threat can be physical or emotional. It can be a real or a perceived threat. Some children operate in a constant state of arousal or hyper-vigilance. This strategy can help the child focus on *staying in the present* and recognizing the difference between feeling safe and feeling threatened.

This is a skill that a child who is anxious or angry can use to reduce the intense emotion that comes with feeling threatened. The process should be relaxing and less structured to encourage free thinking.

Materials • A Safe Place handout
• Paper and Drawing utensils

Process 1. Begin by discussing the terms "safe" and "unsafe." You can use the following script to start the discussion:

→ "Today we are going to think about what the word "safe" means to us. When we are safe, we feel relaxed and calm. We are not thinking about what's bothering us, or worrying about anything that's happened in the past, or will happen next."

2. Feel free to look up the word on the internet, or in a dictionary together.

3. Present the handout and complete Question 1. Discuss the personal meaning of the word safe. You may share what your idea of feeling safe is to get the child started.

→ *Note: Be mindful that children who have experienced trauma may not see the same level of safety in the common places that you may describe (i.e. – home, bedroom, etc.)

4. Move on to Questions 2, 3 and 4.

5. Help the child visualize himself/herself in their own safe place and draw it in the box on the handout.

6. Discuss specific things that help the child feel safe in his/her Safe Place.

A Safe Place (continued)

Variations
- Small Group – Have a small group of children complete the handout and share/process their answers together supportively.

- Situational – Identify a specific place or time when the child is noticeably struggling with feeling unsafe. Alter the exercise so that it applies to only the specific situation.

A Safe Place

1. What does feeling safe mean to you?

   _____

   _____

2. What does feeling unsafe mean to you?

   _____

   _____

3. Things that I don't want to think about when I'm trying to feel safe:

   1. _____

   2. _____

   3. _____

4. Things I need to remember when I'm trying to feel safe:

   1. Focus on what's happing "right now"_____

   2. _____

   3. _____

Draw You in Your Safe Place

Physical Strategies

Animal Stretches

Purpose   This strategy can be used as a preventative exercise, or as a coping skill. When the body is physically stressed, it helps to engage large muscle groups on both sides of the body and move them in smooth, patterned and repetitive motions. For optimal outcomes, this strategy should be taught while the child is calm so that he/she can utilize this skill in a stressed state to prevent further escalation.

Materials   • Animal Stretch Worksheet and drawing utensils

Process   1. Present the child with the worksheet and let him/her know that you are going to be doing some stretches that look like animal movements. Ask the child to choose one of the animals listed on the worksheet.

2. Ask the child to draw the animal and how it moves in the blank space provided.

3. After the child has drawn his/her animal, use the following script to describe the process of the animal stretch.

→ "We are going to pretend that you are the character you have chosen from the handout. Take a deep breath, close your eyes and imagine how your character looks, moves, and sounds. First, imagine how your character moves, now move your body in the same way. Take another deep breath and hold the movement as I count to 5..... 1, 2, 3, 4, 5. Now relax your muscles and take one last deep breath."

4. Repeat this process until the desired calming effects have been achieved. You may want to ask the child to rate on a scale of 1-10 how tense their muscles feel at the beginning of the exercise and then ask them to re-rate how tense they feel after the exercise.

5. Feel free to choose more than one animal to try.

Variations   • This activity can be utilized for small groups or classrooms to start, end or transition from one activity to another, promoting a calm relaxed environment.

• Use the internet to find a video clip of the animal the child has chosen to see how the animal moves.

Animal Stretches

Pick one of the animals and draw it moving in the blank box below.

Emotional Strategies

The second phase of self-regulation requires the skills to label emotions accurately and express them in healthy ways. In addition to these two skills, the strategies contained in this chapter also address the concept of emotional control. It is important for a child to understand that he/she has the ability to control and moderate the expression of his/her emotions.

To increase the chance of success, be sure that the child has some well-developed physical regulation skills before getting too far into the emotional regulation skills. Additionally, we do not recommend attempting to implement the emotional strategies when a child is upset. These strategies were designed to be utilized when the child is physically calm. If the child is physically upset, first use a physical strategy to help the child return to a calm baseline.

Emotional Strategies

You Can't Make Me Laugh

Purpose   Children struggling with self-regulation often do not understand the power they have over their own emotions. This strategy is designed to show children that they themselves have control over their own emotional responses. Others do not dictate how we feel or behave. We have the ability to control our own emotions and behaviors. Understanding this concept is critical for the development of self-regulation.

Materials   • You Can't Make Me Laugh Worksheet

Process   This strategy is to be used when the child is calm and in a good frame of mind to learn.

1. Use the handout and the following script to introduce this activity:

→ "Today we are going to play a game. We are going to try to make each other other laugh. We will not be able touch each other or say anything that is inappropriate. We can tell jokes, say funny words, or make funny faces. We will take turns. First, I will try to make you laugh, and then you will try to make me laugh. When I try to make you laugh, I want you to try not to laugh and when you try to make me laugh, I am going to try not to laugh."

2. After a few rounds, you begin to discuss how you are able to control yourself when the other person is trying to make you laugh. You might say:

→ "Wow, I wonder how you were able to keep from laughing at those funny things I was doing. How did you do that?"

→ Lead the child to figure out that they were making a conscious decision to control their emotions. Maybe they were thinking of something else, or ignoring you. Use the space provided on the handout to write down the different strategies the child used. This is valuable information to discuss with them and build upon to increase self-regulation.

3. After processing the strategies say, "What if we had changed the game to where we were trying to make each other Angry? Would we be able to use the same strategies to control our emotions?" Process this situation utilizing the strategies the child identified.

You Can't Make Me Laugh (continued)

Process   4. End the exercise by reinforcing the fact that we control our own emotions and behaviors. Connect the lesson to real-life examples. Stress that others cannot make us feel happy, sad, scared, or angry unless we choose to. We have the power!

Variations   • Small group – Split into groups of two and complete the exercise. Share strategies and process together as a group.

   • If you are lacking in comedy skills, or feel uncomfortable with trying to make a child laugh, you can replace that portion of the activity with watching a funny video clip, possibly from Youtube™, together while trying not to laugh. With this variation, you can also count how many times the child laughs the first time you watch the video. Then repeat the exercise with the same video at a later time and discuss how he/she was able to laugh less the second time.

You Can't Make Me Laugh

Take turns using funny words, stories, faces or actions to try to get each other to laugh.

Time limit:
Each person gets 30 seconds to get the other to laugh.

Rules:
1. No touching or invading personal space during this game
2. Keep words and actions appropriate
3. Have fun!

Strategies used:

1. _____

2. _____

3. _____

4. _____

5. _____

Emotional Strategies

Feelings Clip Art

Purpose   An important step in helping children become better at regulating emotions is being able to identify emotions accurately. This strategy teaches children how to identify, express, and discuss emotions.

Materials   • Computer with MS Word™ or an equivalent program with access to Clip Art
• Feelings Clip Art sample worksheet

Process   1. Sit down at the computer together and introduce this strategy by saying something like:

→ "Today we are going to explore some different pictures and see what they might mean to us. We are going to try to match pictures with feelings we've had lately."

2. Open MS Word™ and ask the child to type the word "Happy" (feel free to also use the different fonts or colors if you and the child feel comfortable doing so). Then say:

→ "Now let's look for some pictures of things that would fit with Happy."

3. Click on Insert Clip Art to begin searching for pictures and ask the child to help you think of things, or key words, to search for that may fit with feeling Happy (birthday, puppy, family, etc.).

4. As the child inserts 2 or 3 pictures, ask the child to describe times when he/she feels this way.

5. Repeat these steps for Worried, Angry, and Sad.

→ **Note: We recommend that you end on a positive note by finding one more Happy Picture.**

Feelings Clip Art (continued)

Variations
- The adult can also participate and model this exercise by choosing pictures and telling stories that indicate how he/she connects the pictures with the emotions. This can help to engage the child in the process.

- Complete the strategy with a small group. Encourage discussion and sharing of experiences.

- The source of the pictures can be something other than Clip Art, such as a website of famous paintings or photographs.

- One may also want to use this strategy to help a child identify and express emotions related to a specific event or situation. You can search for things that trigger similar feelings as those experienced during the situation or event. You can also illustrate how we can feel more than one emotion about the same event.

Feelings Clip Art

Happy

Worried

Angry

Sad

Emotional Strategies

The Emotional Safe

Purpose   Children who display extreme behaviors often struggle with how to process and express very intense emotions. In order to deal with intense emotions effectively, one must first develop the self-regulatory skills that are necessary for healthy expression.

This strategy is designed to help the child keep those emotions that he/she is not yet prepared to cope with at bay. Then, once the child has developed the necessary self-regulation skills, he/she will be able to re-visit the intense emotion and cope with it in a healthy way.

→ **Note: The object of this strategy is NOT to bury or avoid intense emotions. It is to keep emotions that the child is not yet prepared to cope with at bay for a short time, until he/she has developed the necessary self-regulation skills to cope in a healthy way.**

Materials
- Emotional Safe Worksheet
- Shoebox
- Writing Utensil

Process   1. Use the Worksheet to begin to discuss the idea of how difficult it can be to cope with very strong emotions. Those intense feelings can disrupt our day and get in the way of making friends or getting our work done. Sometimes the feelings are so strong that we may not be able to cope with them right now. Some of these feelings may even be so strong that we need help to process or talk about them.

2. On the Worksheet, right down the Event and the Thoughts, Feelings and Behaviors associated with the Event connected to the intense emotion. It is also important to rate the intensity of the Feelings.

3. List the skills, or keys, that you think will help the child be able to cope with this intense emotion effectively. For example, you may draw on Assumption #2 and recommend that the child masters a physical calming skill before revisiting this difficult situation.

The Emotional Safe (continued)

Purpose   4. Discuss the importance of "locking" this situation away for now. Cut off the bottom portion of the page containing the keys and then fold up the rest of the paper.

5. Now use the shoebox, or container to create the Safe. You can decorate the box to look like a Safe. **Be sure to remind the child that this is only a temporary holding place for the intense emotion.** You may also talk about the double-meaning of the word Safe in this strategy. The Safe is a place to keep the emotion secure, and the process of storing it away temporarily also helps keep everyone safe in the process.

6. Place the folded paper in the Safe and schedule your time to work on the skills you identified.

Variations   • This strategy can also be used when a child repeatedly has difficulty controlling intense emotions that inhibit the child from accomplishing daily tasks or that impact the child's ability to complete activities of daily living.

• The counselor, or teacher, may create one Safe Place for everyone to use. Lay out the worksheets next to the container. Then anyone can write down something that is bothering them. It may be helpful if they don't want to, or don't know how to cope with the problem right now. The child may just need to get it "off of their chest" for the moment, so they can manage their day without stressing about it. The teacher, or counselor, could then review these with the students at a scheduled time.

The Emotional Safe

Event:

_____

_____

Thought:

_____

_____

Feeling:

_____

_____

Behaviors:

_____

_____

Cut here ··

Keys:

1. _____

2. _____

3. _____

Emotional Strategies

Emotional Rain Gauge

Purpose Individuals that struggle with self-regulation have a difficult time identifying and processing their emotions in order to work through them effectively. This often results in the accumulation of stress and anxiety. The stress continues to build and will take its toll physically, emotionally and cognitively. This strategy is designed to illustrate the idea that stress is cumulative and will continue to build if it's not identified and worked through.

Materials
- Emotional Rain Gauge worksheet
- Writing utensil

Process

1. Use the handout to introduce this strategy. You might say something like:

   → "Do you know what a rain gauge is? It's a container that has marks on it to measure how much it has rained. After it rains, we usually check to see how much it rained, and then we dump it out so it's ready for the next rain."

   → "We need to do the same kind of thing with the feelings and problems that bother us."

2. Begin to identify stressors that may be affecting the child and list them on the blank lines. As you list each stressor, color in one section of the rain gauge in the picture.

3. As you continue to add stressors, discuss how difficult it must be to have all of these worries.

4. When the gauge fills up, begin to discuss options for bringing the level back down. We can bring our stress levels down by using:

   → Physical strategies to calm down and relax

   → Emotional strategies to express the feelings in healthy ways

   → Cognitive strategies to engage in effective problems solving

Emotional Rain Gauge (continued)

Variations
- Ask the child draw his or her own rain gauge picture using a computer program like MS Paint™ instead of, or in addition to, using the worksheet.

- In addition to the rain gauge on the computer, or on paper, use a plastic container with simple measurement lines drawn on it. As you add stressors, fill the container up with water to the corresponding measurement line. Ask the child to pick the container up and hold it for a period of time as you add stressors. Point out how "heavy" these stressors can be to carry around.

Emotional Rain Gauge

Stressors:

1. _____

2. _____

3. _____

4. _____

5. _____

6. _____

Emotional Strategies

Emotional Knots

Purpose   Children struggling to express their emotions in healthy ways must first learn to identify and label their feelings accurately. This can be difficult, especially when the situations are complicated, or when we experience different, or even conflicting feelings about the same event. This strategy is designed to draw attention to the process of sorting out complex feelings and identifying them appropriately.

Materials   • 4 colors of yarn, shoe laces, or pipe-cleaner

Process   1. Tie the different colored pieces of yarn into a loosely knotted tangled ball.

2. Use the worksheet and the tangled ball of yarn to introduce this strategy. You might say something like:

→ "Sometimes when things happen around us, we don't know how to feel about them. It can be confusing. Our feelings may get all tangled up and it's hard to sort them out, just like this tangled ball of yarn. Sometimes we need help to make sense of it all. Let's read this short story about Laura and Mary."

3. Read the short story on the worksheet together.

4. Identify a recent event in the child's life that either you or the child believes has been difficult for the child to sort out or express his/her feelings about. Help the child put the event into words in the space provided on the worksheet.

5. Help the child identify the feelings he/she may have experienced during or after the event. Write the feelings in the spaces provided.

6. Present the child with the tangled ball of yarn. Begin to process each of the feelings identified one at a time. Using the color Key, disentangle the colored yarn that corresponds to each of the emotions you process together.

Variation   • Small Group – If there are issues between children, the entangled pieces of yarn can represent individual children within the situation. This can be a way to process an event that seems complicated. Assign each child involved to a color of yarn that is in the tangled knot. As you unravel the knot one color at a time, each child will have a chance to tell their side of the story and the feelings they experienced in the situation. The goal is to promote understanding.

Emotional Knots

Short Story

Laura and Mary were best friends. Mary lived on the same street as Laura and they went to the same school. They played together almost every day for three years. Then one day, when they were in the 4th grade, Mary told Laura that she was moving away. Later that day, Laura began to cry. She decided to talk with her Mother about it. As they talked, they found out that Laura was having lots of different feelings. Here are some of the things she was feeling and why:

Sad ....She thought she was losing a friend

Angry............She thought her friend was leaving her or being taken away

Scared ....She thought she wouldn't be able to find a friend like Mary again

Once Laura and her Mother figured out how Laura was feeling, they could talk about each one of her feelings. Once we know what our feelings are, we can figure out what to do next.

Your Story

What happened in your story?

_____

_____

_____

What feelings are in the story?

1. _____ 2. _____ 3. _____ 4. _____

Color Key

Primary Feelings: Red = Angry • Blue = Sad • Green = Happy • Yellow = Scared/Worried
Other Feelings: Grey = Guilt/Shame • Orange = Surprise

Emotional Strategies

Emotional Overflow

Purpose Children struggling with self-regulation often let their emotions build up inside them to a level that becomes impossible to contain. They reach a point where the emotions burst out in ways that can be destructive or harmful. This strategy is designed to illustrate how emotions that are "stuffed" away can build up and explode.

Materials
- Pitcher of water
- Drinking glass
- Shallow pan
- Emotional Overflow worksheet

Process

1. Use the materials and the worksheet to introduce this strategy. You might say something like:

   → "Sometimes when we get angry or worried, we keep it in and don't tell anyone about it. Let's look at this story about Jose to see what can happen."

2. Set the drinking glass in the shallow pan. Fill the pitcher with water. Tell the child that the drinking glass represents Jose and that the water represents his Anger.

3. Read the story about Jose's Day together and follow the instructions. Pour water from the pitcher into the glass each time you see the word "pour" in the story.

4. After the drinking glass overflows, be sure to make the connection between the anger and stress building up inside Jose and the water building up in the drinking glass.

5. Read the story about Jose's Better Day and follow the instructions.

6. Process the discussion questions together. Identify concrete examples of ways the child can express his/her feelings in healthy ways (talking about it, drawing, exercising, music, etc.).

Emotional Overflow

Jose's Day

Jose is an 8-year-old boy. He is in the 3rd grade. Last night he did not sleep very well. He woke up a lot in the night (pour). When he was getting ready for school he couldn't find the shirt he wanted to wear that day (pour). When he got on the bus, the only seat left open was at the back of the bus and he feels car-sick when he sits back there (pour). When he got to school, he realized he forgot to bring his homework that was due (pour). At recess he got hit in the face with the ball by accident while they were playing soccer (pour).

Jose was getting full of anger and stress (pour until the glass is full). Then when they were lining up for lunch, a girl in Jose's class named Lauren accidently bumped into Jose. Jose's container is full and overflows. He yells and screams at Lauren, then pushes her down (pour to indicate the emotional overflow). All of the anger and stress that had built up inside Jose came out on Lauren.

Jose's Better Day

Jose is an 8-year-old boy. He is in the 3rd grade. Last night he did not sleep very well. He woke up a lot in the night (pour). Jose told his mother and she made sure he had an extra scoop of cereal to help him feel better (pour some of the water in the glass back out). When he was getting ready for school he couldn't find the shirt he wanted to wear that day (pour). He told his dad he was getting mad because he couldn't find his shirt. His dad helped him find it (pour some of the water back out). When he got on the bus, the only seat left open was at the back of the bus and he feels car-sick when he sits back there (pour). When he got to school, he realized he forgot to bring his homework that was due (pour). He told his teacher about it and she said he could bring it in the next day (pour some water back out). At recess he did not get picked to play on the soccer team he wanted to be on (pour). He asked the kids if they could switch teams tomorrow and they agreed (pour some water back out).

Then when they were lining up for lunch, a girl in Jose's class named Lauren accidently bumped into Jose. Jose calmly told Lauren to please watch where she was going.

Questions:

1. What do you think helped Jose's day go better this time?
2. Are there things that you can do to let your feelings out little by little so they don't build up and explode?

Emotional Strategies

Free Healthy Expression

Purpose   Children who struggle with self-regulation often have difficulty expressing the feelings they have in healthy ways. This strategy is purposefully less structured. Genuine, meaningful emotional expression is often very personal. This strategy is designed to help children explore their options for healthy emotional expression.

Materials
- Free Healthy Expression Worksheet
- Writing utensil

Process

1. Introduce this strategy by saying something like:

   → "Our emotions like Anger, Sadness, Fear, and Happiness can be expressed in either healthy or unhealthy ways. For example, talking to someone or drawing a picture of your anger would be a healthy way to express it. Yelling and hitting someone because we are angry would be an unhealthy way to express the feeling. We are to going figure out some healthy ways that you can express your feelings."

2. Use the worksheet to begin to identify the child's areas of interest. You may want to share some of your areas of interest, or other common healthy ways to express our feelings such as sports, art, music, reading, play, writing, etc.

3. Help the child understand that one of the best ways we have to express our feelings is talking with someone else about it. However, we can also use activities to express our feelings.

4. Complete the lower portion of the worksheet by identifying specific actions that the child will take to express each emotion in a healthy way. Try to incorporate the child's personal interests in the activities.

5. Role-play the situations together to make sure they are reasonable, healthy, and make a good fit. Also discuss the preventative value of frequently engaging in activities that allow for healthy expression. They can help keep stress levels low and help prevent the build-up of unpleasant emotions.

6. Ask the child to practice his/her expressive skills and report back to you on how it went. Make adjustments as appropriate.

Free Healthy Expression (continued)

Variations
- Use the internet to research the child's interests and ways others have expressed their emotions. Cyberspace is a place where many children these days express their feelings. This may be a great opportunity to caution the child about the dangers of sharing too much in cyberspace.

- Small Group – Use the group to help brainstorm different ideas for healthy expression. Encourage creativity and the incorporation of each child's areas of interest.

Free Healthy Expression

What are some things you are interested in?

1. _____

2. _____

3. _____

4. _____

Healthy ways I can Express my:

ANGER

1. *Talk with someone about it*

2. _____

3. _____

SADNESS

1. *Talk with someone about it*

2. _____

3. _____

FEAR/WORRY

1. *Talk with someone about it*

2. _____

3. _____

HAPPINESS

1. *Share it with someone*

2. _____

3. _____

Cognitive Strategies

The strategies contained in this chapter build on the skills developed in the previous chapters and require a higher level of ability. To be ready for this level of skill, the child should have well-developed physical calming skills, be able to identify and express emotions in healthy ways, and accept that he/she can exercise control over his/her own physical and emotional responses.

It is important to communicate that not every child is ready for these higher level strategies. In particular, younger children and those who have significant cognitive or developmental delays may not have the ability to comprehend the concepts contained in this chapter. However, we have learned that having well-developed physical and emotional regulation skills will give the child a better chance of progressing into higher level cognitive regulation and more advanced self-directed problem-solving.

Cognitive Strategies

Don't Take the Bait

Purpose   Children with self-regulation issues often have difficulty resisting the impulse to react to the behaviors of others. Learning to moderate their responses to external events will improve self-control and reduce the likelihood of negative behaviors. This strategy uses the analogy of fishing to illustrate the child's ability to choose their responses carefully and avoid being "hooked" and reacting to the provocation of others.

This strategy can be particularly useful with children who:
→ are easily distracted by the negative actions of others
→ are easily provoked
→ tend to retaliate with negative behaviors
→ have become targets of negative behavior
→ have a strong need to "get even"

Materials   • Don't Take the Bait Worksheet
   • Writing utensil

Process   1. Use the Worksheet to begin to discuss the idea of how others behave in ways that we can't control, but we can control how we respond. Relate this concept to the act of fishing. Convey to the child that he/she is like the fish who is trying to avoid being "hooked" by responding negatively to the provoking behaviors of others.

2. Discuss recent examples of the child being "baited" and "hooked" by others. Emphasize how those situations turned out.

3. Identify specific behaviors or actions that the child has particular difficulty dealing with. List these on the fishing poles and down the fishing lines leading to the hooks.

4. Ask the child to draw himself/herself as a fish in the space indicated. The child (fish) must get past the 3 hooks to get to "safety." Process how he/she might be able to avoid each of the "baited hooks."

5. Remind the child of times that he/she has been able to successfully avoid the hooks. Draw upon those successes to process and develop strategies for the future.

Don't Take the Bait (continued)

Variations
- Use a real fishing pole and tape or a magnet to illustrate how it might look when others "cast" negative behaviors toward us. Write a negative behavior on a small piece of paper cast it out close to the child. Discuss healthy ways to respond to the negative behavior.

- Group exercise: Have the children divide up into two groups. One group will be the fishermen and one group will be the fish. Play out the experience while discussing how the fish can navigate through all of the different "baits." You can also incorporate ideas like the benefits of staying in a group or staying focused on the end goal.

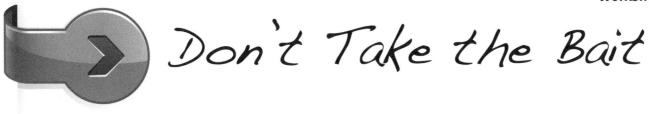

Don't Take the Bait

Draw yourself as a fish in the water below. Write the behaviors on the poles and down the lines that others are doing to "bait" you into reacting and "hooking" yourself. Process how you can get past the hooks and make it to safety. Some hints are written on the seaweed.

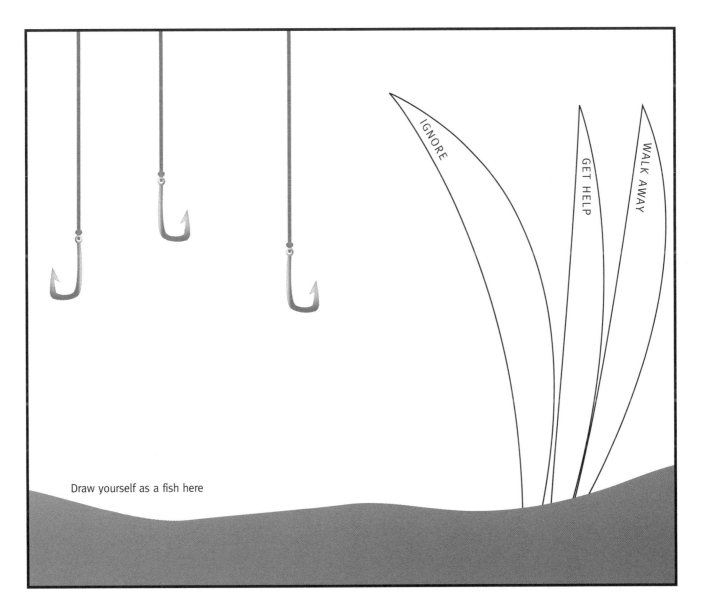

IGNORE

GET HELP

WALK AWAY

Draw yourself as a fish here

Cognitive Strategies

Defiance Trap

Purpose Children struggling with self-regulation often have difficulty complying with rules and limits. A critical part of self-regulation is understanding that one's own actions can dictate the amount of freedom they are granted by parents, teachers and others in authority.

This strategy is designed to be used with children who struggle with following the rules, and it illustrates the direct relationship between the child's behaviors and the amount of freedom and trust he/she is given by others.

Materials
- Defiance Trap handout
- Writing utensil

Process
1. Use the worksheet to begin to discuss the relationship between one's own actions and the amount of trust and freedom they currently have. For example you may say:

   → "Many children who struggle with rules seem to be unhappy with the rules. They tell me that the rules are unfair and that they can't do what they want to do when they want to do it. They tell me that they want more freedom. But is seems to me that the more they push against the rules, the less freedom they end up with."

2. Discuss what personal freedom is and how it allows people to have more choices and more "space" to do what they want because others trust them more. When individuals break rules, they tend to draw a lot of attention from authority figures and have more people telling them what to do, rather than less. Conversely, those that operate within the limits, have more freedom to do as they please, and sometimes even receive special freedoms.

3. Discuss how quicksand is deceiving. It looks solid and safe, but it becomes unstable and dangerous when stepped in. Similarly, it is easy to mistakenly think that the way to get more freedom is to "break through" all of the rules. However, similar to quicksand, the more one struggles, the worse things get.

Defiance Trap (continued)

Process

4. On the worksheet make a connection between the child's current behavioral situation and the quicksand. Help the child identify and list the thoughts and rule-breaking behaviors that seem to act like the quicksand, keeping them "trapped" and reducing the amount of freedom they have.

→ **Note: Be sure to reinforce the idea that it's the child's own behavior, not the rules themselves, that dictate the outcome.**

5. Identify the realistic freedoms that the child would like to earn. Communicate that these freedoms are within reach based on consistent compliance. You may want to formulate a more specific plan with timelines and steps that the child can take to reach the goals.

Variations

- Finger-trap – The Chinese finger-trap game can be used to illustrate how impulsive struggling results in further restriction. Help the child connect this feeling to the results of continued defiance.

- Search for videos and information on the internet to illustrate how quicksand works.

- Group exercise – Use any game where breaking the rules leaves the individual worse off than if he/she would have followed the rules.

Defiance Trap

First, draw yourself in the trap below.
Next, list the Freedoms or Privileges you would like to earn:

1. _____

2. _____

3. _____

Write in thoughts or rule-breaking behaviors that are keeping you from reaching your goals:

1. _____

   _____

2. _____

   _____

3. _____

   _____

Cognitive Strategies

Finish Your Thoughts

Purpose This strategy is designed to increase the child's awareness of the connection between thoughts and emotions. Children who regulate poorly often feel like their behaviors and emotions are out of their control. They may not have been taught that the thoughts they choose to think significantly impact their feelings.

We think in words, and the words we choose to think can impact what emotion we experience and also how intense the emotion feels. Learning this concept provides the understanding necessary for control and the motivation for creating change.

Materials
- Finish Your Thoughts Worksheets
- Writing utensil

Process
1. Use the Finish Your Thoughts 1 handout and this script to introduce the strategy:

   → "We will look at a few short stories today about other children. The stories have blanks that we need to fill in. The first time we go through the story, we will fill in the blanks with "Extreme" words. We will then see how we think the main character might feel based on the story."

2. Complete Section 1 of the handout together by filling in the blanks with the words from the Word Bank in Section 1. Together, name the Feeling(s) that Sara is experiencing and how intense the Feeling(s) seem.

3. Next, complete Section 2 the same way. To transition you might say something like:

   → "Now we are going to go through the story again, but select different words to fill in the blanks."

4. Process the difference between the two outcomes. The only differences in the stories are the descriptor words. Draw attention to the difference in the intensity of the feelings between the two stories, and also point out that Sara has a choice about which words she thinks.

5. If time allows, you can go through the Finish Your Thoughts 2 handout.

Finish Your Thoughts (continued)

Variations

- After the child becomes familiar with the strategy, he/she can create his/her own short story with blanks to fill in using the Finish Your Thoughts 3 handout.

- Small Group – Select members of the group to act out the situation in front of the group. Assign one to use the Extreme words in their thoughts and another to use more moderate words. Process the connection between the characters' thoughts and their feelings/actions.

Finish Your Thoughts

Sara's Math Test

Section 1

Math is difficult for Sara. She finds out that she has a test tomorrow in Math class. She starts thinking:

"I _____ Math. I am _____ at it. I _____ do _____ on my Math tests. There is _____ I am going to pass."

WORD BANK:
hate   terrible   always   horrible   no way

Feeling(s): _____

On a scale of 1-10, how much does Sara feel this way? _____

Section 2

"I _____ Math. I am _____ at it. I _____ do _____ on my Math tests. There is _____ I am going to pass."

WORD BANK:
sometimes struggle in   okay   sometimes   okay   a good chance

Feeling(s): _____

On a scale of 1-10, how much does Sara feel this way? _____

Finish Your Thoughts

John's Recess

Section 1

John is a new student and he is getting ready to go out for recess.
He starts thinking:

"People _____ want to play with me. _____ likes me. I'm

_____ at meeting new people. This is going to be _____."

WORD BANK:
never   nobody   horrible   awful

Feeling(s): _____

On a scale of 1-10, how much does John feel this way? _____

Section 2

"People _____ want to play with me. _____ like me. I'm

_____ at meeting new people. This is going to be _____."

WORD BANK:
sometimes   some people   okay   fine

Feeling(s): _____

On a scale of 1-10, how much does John feel this way? _____

Finish Your Thoughts

Template

Section 1

Situation: _____

_____

I start thinking: " _____

_____ "

WORD BANK:
_____ _____ _____ _____

Feeling(s): _____

On a scale of 1-10, how strongly would you feel this way? _____

Section 2

Situation: _____

_____

I start thinking: " _____

_____ "

WORD BANK:
_____ _____ _____ _____

Feeling(s): _____

On a scale of 1-10, how strongly would you feel this way? _____

The Domino Effect

Purpose Those who struggle with self-regulation often have difficulty understanding the fact that they can control their own emotional and behavioral outcomes for events that take place in their lives. They also have difficulty with being pro-active in stopping a negative chain of events from spiraling out of control.

This strategy is designed to illustrate how quickly and easily one can find themselves at the end of a string of negative events. The goal is to become aware of one's ability to interrupt the chain of events, implement a pro-active choice, and change the outcome.

Materials • Approximately 20 dominos
• Domino Effect worksheet

Process 1. With the Domino Effect worksheet, sit down with the child to process a recent situation where the child may have had several negative behaviors or interactions. Use the worksheet to identify how this negative chain of events began. Write the activating event in the appropriate section and cut it out. This will serve as the beginning of the domino chain.

2. Record the end result in the appropriate box. Cut it out and place it where you want the chain to end.

3. As you begin to set up the dominos in a line connecting the two cards, discuss how the child's decisions, or actions, along the way keep things continuing down a negative track. Point out that if something is not done to change this direction, it will likely continue to the negative outcome. Complete the line and knock down the domino chain to illustrate this point.

4. List as many decision points as you can on the worksheet. Decision points are times along the way where the child could have been pro-active and stopped the negative chain of events from continuing and created a new direction.

5. Write in a positive outcome on the worksheet and cut it out. Place it in a different area than the negative outcome.

The Domino Effect (continued)

Purpose

6. Identify a decision point that could have led to the pro-active outcome. Re-route the domino trail based on the positive decision that leads to the new outcome. Be sure to point out that this takes place when a pro-active decision is made and remind the child of who controls these decision points. Let the child knock down the domino line to illustrate the chain of events.

Variations

- Use a space or two in-between a couple of the dominos along the chain toward the negative outcome to put in specific decision points that can stop a negative chain of events. Use the decision point boxes to list interventions, cut them out, and put them in place of a domino to disrupt the chain by creating a large enough gap so that the domino chain stops on the paper. You can also use these decision points to "reroute" the domino chain to a positive outcome.

- Group effect – Use the dominos to show how one change in the system (group or classroom) can impact the rest of the people (students, group members, teachers, family members) in both negative and positive ways. Use the dominos to illustrate how a small event like knocking over one domino, can lead to a long chain of events that impact the entire group. Discuss the numerous ways that the chain could be re-routed or interrupted pro-actively to create a positive outcome for the group.

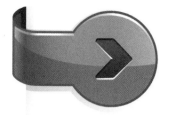

Domino Effect

Let's look at how you can control the outcome.

Activating Event	End Result (Negative)

Decision points (interventions)

1. _____

2. _____

3. _____

4. _____

Positive Pro-active Ending

Cognitive Strategies

Magnetic Thoughts

Purpose Those individuals that struggle with self-regulation often have well-established belief systems that are unhealthy. The stronger a belief becomes, the more difficult it is to modify. One reason for this is that the established belief attracts information that supports itself and ignores/rejects information that is contrary.

For example, if a child holds the belief, "I'm worthless" and they get a "C" on a test, he/she may think "That's horrible. I'm stupid." These thoughts would be attracted to the negative belief of being worthless. The teacher may even say that this test was very difficult and that a "C" is okay and it's likely that he/she would "do better on the next test." This positive statement would be ignored/rejected because it doesn't match or fit with the child's established belief system. This strategy is designed to illustrate this process.

Materials
- Magnet
- All-plastic paperclips
- Metal paperclips
- Magnetic Thoughts Worksheet

Process
1. Use the magnet and the two different types of paperclips to show how it attracts metal, but not plastic.

2. In the space provided on the worksheet, write down an established belief that the child may be struggling with. Common unhealthy beliefs include:

→ I'm not good enough
→ Nobody likes me
→ Everyone is against me
→ I can't do anything right
→ New things are scary and unsafe
→ I have to get even
→ Everything must always be fair

3. Indicate that the magnet represents the belief, and to a certain degree, the child.

4. Write down some events or thoughts that could reinforce or strengthen the unhealthy belief in the column on the worksheet labeled Metal.

Magnetic Thoughts (continued)

Purpose

5. Write down some healthy/positive statements, which are likely to be ignored, in the column on the worksheet labeled Plastic.

6. Cut out the boxes and attach them to the corresponding paperclips. Scatter these around the tabletop. Remind the child that the magnet represents him/her and his/her beliefs.

7. Move the magnet around the tabletop and discuss how certain events/thoughts are attracted and they "chain" together to make the unhealthy belief larger and more powerful. Also discuss how the healthy thoughts/events are passed over and ignored.

8. After moving the magnet around through the paperclips, point out that what the child ended up with was all of the negative information that feeds the unhealthy belief.

9. You can then discuss the positive statements that were ignored and help the child use this information to challenge the unhealthy belief and pay more attention to this information in the future.

Variations

• Go through the strategy again. This time attaching the healthy thoughts/events to the metal paperclips and the unhealthy thoughts/events to the plastic paperclips. Replace the unhealthy established belief with a healthy established belief to show that healthy thoughts can work the same way.

• Small Group – Complete the exercise using everyone in the group to help generate several healthy and unhealthy examples. It can be very powerful to have others help develop positive statements to counteract the negative beliefs and to help provide concrete examples/evidence.

Magnetic Thoughts

Our thoughts can be like magnets.
Be careful about what thoughts you choose to think.

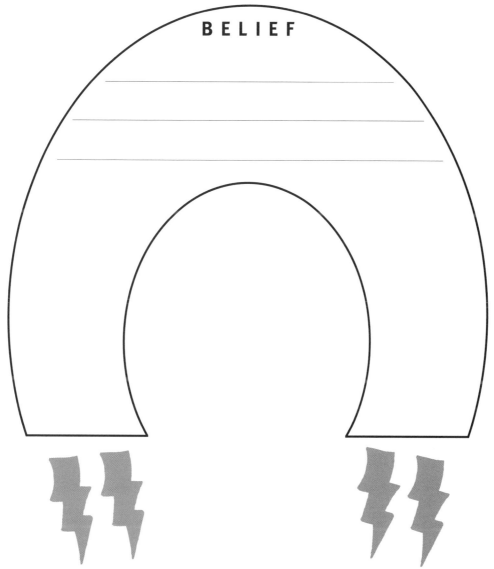

BELIEF

Metal	Plastic

|

Stressor Detection Radar

Purpose Individuals who have difficulty with self-regulation often over-respond or under-respond to stressors in their lives. The goal of this strategy is to improve the child's ability to recognize, appropriately assess and respond to stressors.

Materials • Stress Detection Radar Worksheet

Process 1. Use the worksheet to introduce this strategy. After making sure the child knows what a radar screen is used for, you may say something like:

→ "A stressor is something that's happening around you that is asking for your attention. It is like something that would show up on a radar screen. Let's try to think of some stressors that are happening in your life right now."

2. Collaborate with the child to develop a list of stressors and write them on the numbered lines. You may encourage the child to elaborate on the identified stressors.

3. We want the child to prioritize the list by importance and intensity. You may say:

→ "We need to think about how important each of these things are right now. Which one do you think needs the most attention first?"

→ Discuss the intensity of the stressors and rank them in order, number one being the most pressing.

4. Write the number of the stressor in the place it should fall on the radar, with the more pressing stressors closer to the middle.

5. If time and the situation allow, you may want to begin problem-solving work on the stressors.

Variations • Print a generic weather map with areas to write in stressors around the child's home town. Storms could represent the stressors on the map.

• Small group – Complete the strategy with the group as the main focus. Identify stressors that would impact the group as a whole (i.e. – state assessments). Then brainstorm as a group to prioritize and discuss ways to cope or prepare.

Stressor Detection Radar

Stressors are things around us that are asking for some attention.

Draw line corresponding to perceived intensity level of the stressors, with those closer to the center being the most intense. Process ways to reduce negative impact and prioritize the stressors

Stressors: _____

_____

_____

_____

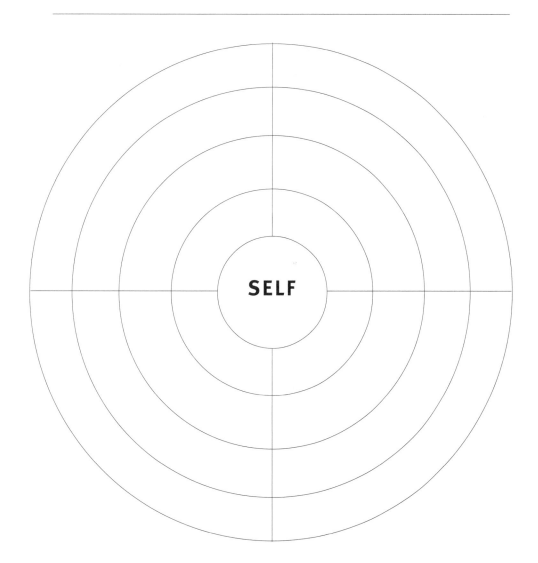

Cognitive Strategies

Shaping Your Thoughts

Purpose   Extreme behaviors and emotions are common with poor self-regulation. Extreme behaviors are often the product of extreme thoughts or beliefs. These beliefs act as "filters" for processing incoming information. This process creates our perception of the incoming information. We tend to "hear" things that match up with our current belief systems, and "reject" things that don't match.

For example, if a child has the belief that he is worthless, he will tend to only pay attention to comments and actions that match with this belief. He will reject, or dismiss, compliments and positive actions from others that are contradictory to his belief of being worthless.

The goal of this strategy is to raise the child's awareness of how our own thoughts and beliefs impact our feelings and behaviors. This strategy may also help identify extreme or unhealthy thoughts the child is having so that they can be modified.

Materials   • Shaping Your Thoughts Worksheets (1, 2 & 3)
• Scissors
• Writing utensil

Process   1. Introduce this strategy by saying something like:

→ "We all have ideas about ourselves, other people, and the world around us. If I say the word "elephant" everyone has ideas about what that means to them. Today we are going to take a look at how our ideas can make us feel certain ways."

2. Locate Worksheets 1 and 2. These worksheets will serve as filters (one for Healthy Beliefs and one for Unhealthy Beliefs).

3. Begin by identifying an Unhealthy thought or belief that the child has been struggling with. Write it at the top of the Unhealthy Filter page and then cut out and discard the Triangles on this Filter page.

4. Generate a few recent events, comments, or situations that the child has had to respond to recently and write them in the triangles on Worksheet 3. It's okay to make these up if the child cannot remember any specific events. Cut out the triangles.

Cognitive Strategies

Shaping Your Thoughts (continued)

Purpose

5. Replay the events together with your Event Shapes and your Filter to see which thoughts "get through" and are going to be remembered.

6. Re-write a more Healthy and Helpful version of the Belief at the top of the Healthy Filter Page. Cut out and discard the Squares. Select recent events, comments, or situations and write them in the squares on Worksheet 3. It's okay to make these up if the child cannot remember any specific events. Cut out these squares.

7. Replay the events together with your Event Shapes and your Filter to see which thoughts "get through" and are going to be remembered based on this Healthy Belief.

Variations

• Use a Shoebox and cut 2 square-shaped holes and 2 triangular-shaped holes in the top. Indicate the Belief Filter you are using (Healthy or Unhealthy). You can do this by taping the Belief to side of the box. Complete the processing exercise and then open the box to see what you have inside. Process how you might feel with only these Comments or Events inside.

• Small Group – Create one box for the group to use with the different filters. Have groups of two identify the Healthy and Unhealthy beliefs.

 *Shaping Your Thoughts*

Unhealthy Filter

Belief:

_____

*Cut out the Triangles.

Square = Healthy Belief or Event   Triangle = Unhealthy Belief or Event

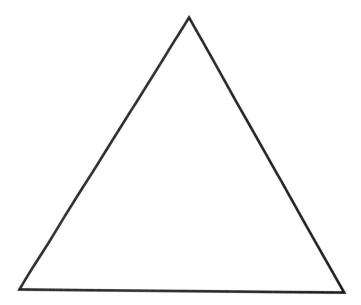

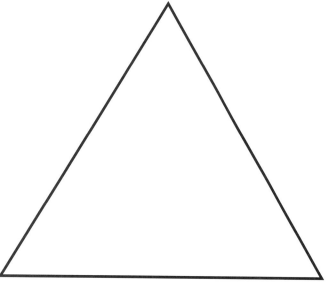

Shaping Your Thoughts

Healthy Filter

Belief:

_____

*Cut out the Squares.

Square = Healthy Belief or Event   Triangle = Unhealthy Belief or Event

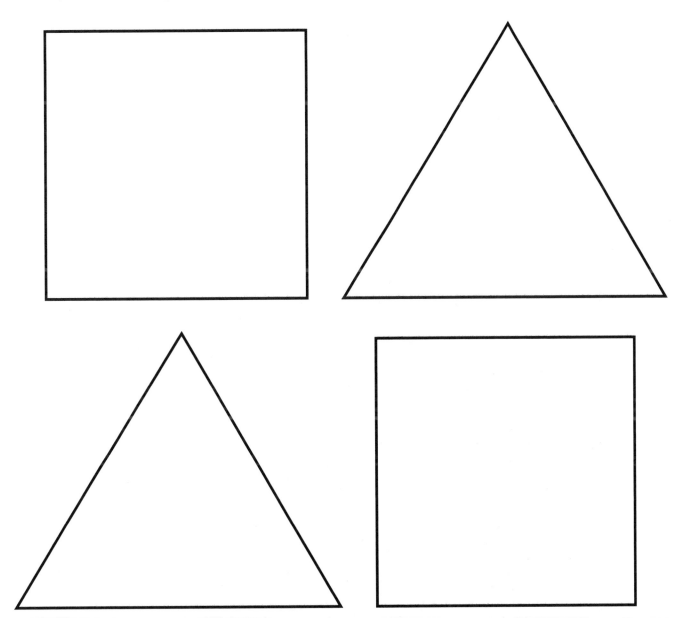

Shaping Your Thoughts

Events, Comments, Situations

Healthy & Helpful

Unhealthy & Not Helpful

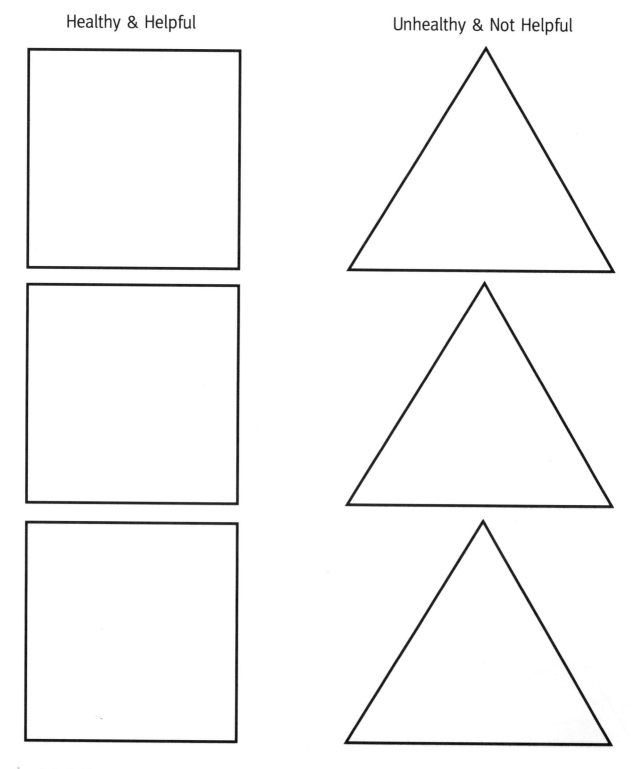

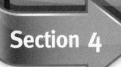

Cognitive Strategies

Problem Solving Remote Control

Purpose   Children who have been struggling to self-regulate often have difficulty slowing down, mindfully reflecting on past situations, and looking ahead to predict the consequences of their choices. This strategy is used to improve the child's self-regulation skills by focusing on his/her ability to slow down and assess specific situations in order to determine the potential consequences relating to his/her actions and learn to make healthy choices.

Materials   • Problem Solving Remote Worksheet

Process   1. Use the worksheet to introduce this strategy. You might say something like:

→ "We are going to use this remote to control time so that we can back up, stop, or go forward and see if there are things that you might want to look at or change."

2. You can have the child "test out" the remote by pressing the Stop or Pause button to fully disengage the child from his/her previous activity. This can be especially helpful if the child is still a little upset about a particular situation or has difficulty with transition.

3. Ask the child to press the Rewind button and identify in his/her own words what happened in the specific situation he/she is struggling with (no right or wrong answers, just get them talking & thinking).

4. Fast-Forward to what might happen if this problem goes without processing, or is handled in another way. List several possible outcomes including both positive and negative.

5. Decide upon "the best" option and press the Play button to role-play the situation together.

Problem Solving Remote Control (continued)

Variations
- Use previously recorded scenes involving choices from movies, or other sources, that can be stopped/paused, rewound, played and fast- forwarded. Use these situations for the discussion of problem-solving alternatives.

- Small Group - Using cardboard and glue, ask each child to cut out the remote control and glue it to a piece of cardboard so that each child has his/her own remote to use during the process.

- Small Group – Assign parts and act out common situations that children struggle with. Use the remote to stop, play, rewind, and fast-forward the scenes while generating discussion and problem-solving.

Problem Solving Remote Control

Situation:

_____

_____

_____

_____

Play...Move at typical speed
Stop/Pause ....Calm Down, Reflect, Think
Fast Forward (FFD) ....Move ahead to see Outcome
Rewind (RWD) ....Back up to Change behaviors

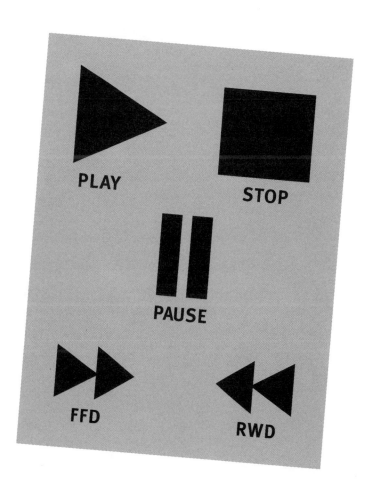

Cognitive Strategies

Grow A Thought

Purpose   This strategy combines the ability to effectively challenge unhealthy thoughts with the ability to cultivate healthy thoughts. It's more difficult to challenge unhealthy thinking when we don't have solid healthy beliefs to draw upon. This strategy utilizes the metaphor of growing a plant to symbolize establishing a healthy core belief. This strategy also encourages self-monitoring.

Materials   • Grow A Thought Worksheet
• Writing utensil

Process   1. Based on your knowledge of the child, attempt to identify a few thoughts or beliefs that you think would be the most helpful for this child to develop. For example: If the child struggles with self-esteem, the thought you might want to grow could be something like "I am a good person."

2. When meeting with the child, begin to introduce the strategy by saying something like:

→ "Today, we are going to plant a thought. Have you ever grown a plant? Planting a thought works in much the same way."

→ "It starts as a seed and it needs food and water to grow. We also have to make sure that weeds don't grow around our plant. The "food" and "water" for our thoughts will be things that we see or hear that can help it to grow. We have to gather the food and water by watching and listening for them."

→ "The "weeds" will be anything that we hear or see that might hurt our plant. These might be other thoughts we have or things people might say."

→ "As we add food and water, we will be able to see our thought plant grow. Remember, when weeds appear we will need to get rid of them."

3. Use the Sample to show the process.

Grow A Thought (continued)

Purpose
4. Help the child choose what thought to Grow. It is difficult to go wrong here. As long as the thought seems related to the child's issues and is positive, you are working in the right direction.

→ Common examples of thoughts to Grow:

→ I am likable

→ I am worthy

→ I am a good helper

→ I can be brave

→ There are lots of good things about me

→ I can _____

5. Discuss how to find food for the thought. You might say something like:

"We will give our thought plant some food today, and the next time we get together to check on it, you will need to have some food and water for it. Keep track of anything you hear or see that might help it grow."

6. Discuss the challenge of weeds. You might say something like:

→ "We will also want to check for any weeds the next time we get together. Keep track of anything that might hurt the thought we planted so we can take care of it."

→ "To remove the weeds, write the negative event in the weed box, and draw the weed next to the plant in pencil. After processing it and comparing it with the food to prove that it's inaccurate, erase the weed."

7. Repeat the process over the next week or so to see the thought reach maturity.

Variations
• Utilize the computer to create a unique plant at different stages of development. Be creative and add flowers or substitute a tree as the plant.

• Combine this Strategy with a physical science experiment involving plant science and watching a "real" plant grow. Draw connections between what is needed to nurture the plant and also the thought.

• Small Group – Encourage the group to share their individual thoughts/plants with the each other. Ask the members to provide some "food/water" for each of the other members to help them get started and grow their plants faster.

Grow A Thought

Food & Water ....Things that help our thought plant grow
Weeds ....Things that keep our thought plant from growing

Seedling

"Food & Water"	"Weeds"

Sprout

"Food & Water"	"Weeds"

Full Plant

"Food & Water"	"Weeds"

Cognitive Strategies

Target Practice

Purpose Individuals that struggle with self-regulation often have difficulty forming a healthy perspective of the events that happen around them. They commonly misinterpret neutral events and the intentions of others. This strategy is designed to illustrate how important it is to accurately interpret the events that happen around us. Our interpretation dictates our emotional and behavioral response, so we want our responses to be accurate.

Materials
- Target Practice Sample
- Target Practice Worksheet
- Pencil

Process
1. Use the sample and the worksheet to help introduce this strategy. Begin by helping the child identify a particular situation that he/she is struggling with.

2. Explain that the "target" on the worksheet has a bulls-eye that represents the most accurate interpretation. The second ring on the target is a moderately inaccurate interpretation, and the last ring represents a very extreme interpretation of the event. See the sample.

3. Identify three possible interpretations of the event that you and the child listed in step one. Like the sample, create one very extreme interpretation for the outer ring, one that is less extreme but still unhealthy for the middle ring, and one that is accurate and healthy for the target's center ring. Write these in the 3 corresponding boxes on the worksheet.

4. Place the paper target on the floor. Ask the child to hold a pencil approximately 3 or 4 feet above the paper. Then ask the child to drop the pencil and try to hit the bulls-eye.

5. After the child drops the pencil, process the interpretation according to where the pencil hit the target. Discuss the intensity of the emotion that would be expressed with each of the different thoughts. Be sure to reinforce that the extreme, inaccurate thoughts would likely result in extreme emotions and behaviors. Repeat this process until all 3 interpretations have been discussed at least once.

Target Practice (continued)

Variations
- Substitute a felt or Velcro target set for the paper and pencil.

- Assign point values to the 3 levels and try to reach 100 points.

- Utilize a bean-bag target system.

Target Practice

Example:

Event – Another child cut in front of you in line.

Everybody is
Against me!

He can't do that.
I'm going to get
even with him.

I can't
control him,
but I can control
myself.
I could let it go,
talk to him, or ask
the teacher.

Target Practice

Example:
Event _____

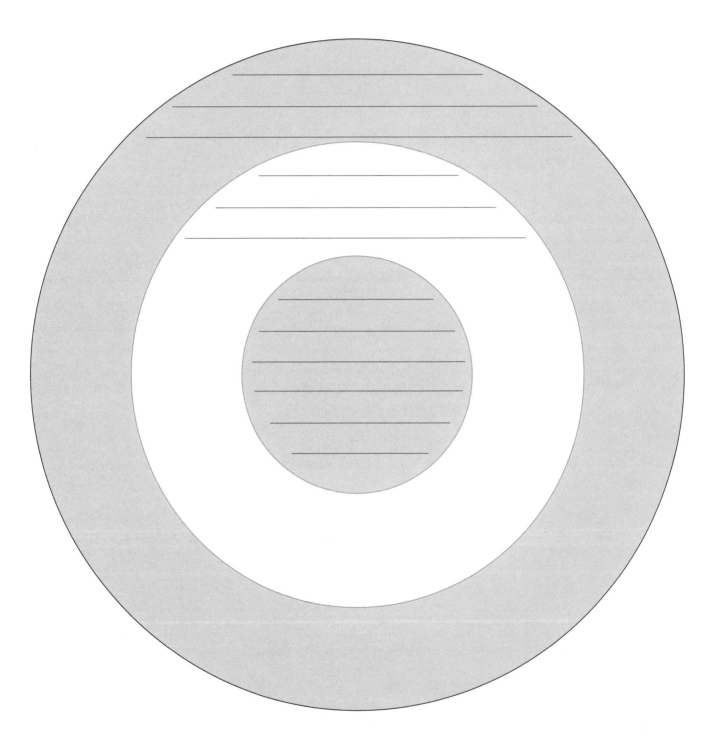

The goals of Self-regulation training are to help children develop and implement physical, emotional, and cognitive skills effectively to cope with most of life's challenges in healthy and pro-active ways. The following 8-session plans serve well as guides, with the understanding that every individual is at a different place with regard to his or her own self-regulation skill development.

One of the major benefits of this approach is its flexibility. The physical, emotional, and cognitive domains provide a natural sequence; however, there is a great deal of freedom in which the strategies are selected and what problems are addressed. You can create tailor-made curricula for children that target several specific problem areas, including those listed across the top of the Problem/Strategy Matrix (p. 14), with this one resource. The authors encourage a dynamic interpretation and execution of these curricula. In other words, feel free to add your own style, incorporate your own favorite interventions, and keep it fun. Make it your own.

Please understand that although this approach is a simple and systematic way of teaching self-regulation skills, human beings are dynamic and can move back and forth between physical, emotional, and cognitive areas of self-regulation within one encounter. For example, a child who has been upset, but with your help is now physically calm, can begin to physically escalate again as you try to move into helping the child express his/her emotions. This would provide an opportunity to help the child recognize that he/she is becoming physically escalated again and that he/she needs to repeat a physical calming strategy in order to calm down before attempting to move forward.

The following section provides an example of how this Self-regulation Training approach easily lends itself to the creation of a curriculum to address a specific issue like Anger.

Sample 8-Session Self-regulation Curriculum for Anger Management

Introduce this journey to the child simply as a chance to learn some life skills together. The two of you will meet eight times for approximately 15 to 30 minutes each session. If possible, complete the Assessment tool (Appendix, p. 101) prior to Session 1 to help you focus your training efforts and gather baseline information.

The following Curriculum is based on a set of self-regulation skills that most children with anger problems benefit from. It may be used as a guide, but please adjust your approach and strategy selection according to the results of the Assessment for the child you are working with.

Before you begin, send home a copy of the Parent letter (p. 103) with the child. The first week is primarily for building engagement in the process and understanding the Physical piece of Self-regulation. The Self-regulation Training Contract (p. 104) helps clarify the goal of your time together and can help provide the motivation for change and engagement.

Session 1

1. Provide the child with a blank folder to keep his/her worksheets in as references. Introduce this journey by saying something like:

→ "Over the next few weeks we are going to get together and try some new things. We will be using some fun activities to help us learn how to control our bodies, our feelings, and our thoughts better. People who learn how to do these things well live longer, are happier and do better in school. Wouldn't we like to live longer, be happier, and do better in school?"

2. Complete the Self-regulation Training Contract based on the information from the Assessment tool. Use this contract to engage the child in the process.

3. Complete the Physical strategy Warning Signs (p. 25) together.

4. Process the experience together and link the activity to real-life situations as much as possible.

5. Assign homework: At the next session, the child will give two examples of situations when he/she was able to recognize his/her warning signs.

Session 2

1. Quickly review the homework assignment from Session 1.

2. Continue to focus on the Physical skills and complete the Melting Freeze (p. 23) strategy together.

3. Introduce the child to the Cooling the Flame (p. 19) exercise and make a plan for this strategy to be available to the child if he/she needs to use it.

4. Process the differences and the similarities in the two calming techniques. Discuss how these strategies can be implemented in real-life situations.

5. Assign homework: Practice Melting Freeze two times before the next session.

The focus for the next two sessions is on feelings identification and the idea that we have control over how we choose to express our emotions, including Anger. Often children struggling with Anger issues only know how to identify and express the feeling of Anger. Therefore it is important to broaden their emotional vocabulary to include other emotions.

Session 3

1. Quickly review the homework assignment from the last session.

2. Complete the strategy Feelings Clipart (p. 40) together.

3. Help the child recognize feelings other than Anger that he/she may be experiencing as a result of real-life situations.

4. Assign homework: Ask the child to bring in one example of a time where he/she recognized his warning signs, identified the feeling(s), and used a physical calming strategy.

Session 4

1. Quickly review and process the homework assignment from the last session.

2. Complete the Emotional Overflow strategy (p. 51) together. Discuss how important it is to be able to express our feelings.

3. Complete the Free Healthy Expression strategy (p. 53) together to help the child identify appropriate emotional outlets.

4. Assign homework: Be prepared to report one time that you were able to express anger/frustration in a healthy way.

The goal for the next two sessions is to increase internal/external awareness and problem-solving strategies. Keep in mind that some children may not be developmentally ready for this stage. If the child is not ready to move into the Cognitive skills, don't force it. Anger can be managed quite well with mastery of the Physical and Emotional skills.

Anger Management and Small Group Core Curricula

Session 5

1. Quickly review and process the homework assignment from the last session.

2. There are several of the Cognitive strategies that are effective for targeting Anger problems. Use the Problem/Strategy Matrix (p. 14) and your information from the Assessment to choose two strategies that fit the child's situation.

3. Complete one of the strategies you've selected. You will complete the second one in the next session.

4. Assign homework: Ask the child to practice or report on something related to the strategy you've completed in this session.

Session 6

1. Quickly review and process the homework assignment from the last session.

2. Complete the 2nd Cognitive strategy you chose for this child.

3. If time allows, ask the child to select a 3rd Cognitive strategy that relates to his/her situation.

4. Assign homework: Ask the child to teach a Physical calming exercise to another person.

The final two sessions focus on putting all of the self-regulation skills together and reinforcing these new behaviors.

Session 7

1. Quickly review and process the homework assignment from the last session.

2. Role-play two of the following events and process them together using the Event Processing Worksheet (p. 105) as a guide:
   a. You are not picked for a team to play in a game at recess and have to sit out
   b. Another child laughs at you for dropping your books on the floor
   c. A child bumps into you while lining up for lunch
   d. You were told "No" when you asked to do something

3. It's important to role-play through each of the strategies selected to insure that the child is able to identify and implement the physical, emotional and cognitive strategies he/she chooses to use. Monitor how the child progresses through each strategy. This will give you valuable information about what concepts may need to be reviewed.

4. Assign homework: Let someone else know how you express Anger in a healthy way. Identify a situation from your life that has happened recently to discuss next time.

Session 8

1. Review the homework assignment from the last session.

2. Use the Event Processing Worksheet (p. 105) to process the real-life example the child brought to the session. Encourage the child to lead as much as he/she is able to.

3. Draw specific attention to the Physical, Emotional, and Cognitive strategies the child decides to implement to cope with the situation. Transfer the child's favorite strategies to the My Self-regulation Strategies worksheet (p. 106) for the child to use as a quick reference.

4. Discuss the progress the child has made over the past few weeks. Complete the Self-regulator Certificate (p. 107) and celebrate the success.

5. Make plans to touch base over the next few weeks to review continued progress. Complete the Assessment Tool to re-assess progress by re-rating the problem areas.

Anger Management and Small Group Core Curricula

Small Group Brief Self-regulation Core Training Curriculum

This brief model is designed to be delivered to a small group of children. It consists of eight sessions lasting 15 to 30 minutes each. The goal is to provide those in the small group with the skills and the language to better manage themselves. We have selected 2 strategies from each of the 3 categories of Self-regulation to incorporate into this core curriculum. Please use this as a guide, but feel free to add strategies based on the unique dynamics of the group.

Before you begin, send home a copy of the Parent letter (p. 103) with each child. The first week is primarily for building engagement in the process and understanding the Physical piece of Self-regulation.

Session 1

1. Provide each child with a blank folder to keep their individual worksheets in a s references. Introduce this 8-session journey by saying something like:

   → "Over the next few weeks we are all going to get together and try some new things. We will be using some fun activities to help us learn how to control our bodies, our feelings, and our thoughts better. People who learn how to do these things well live longer, are happier and do better in school. Wouldn't we all like to live longer, be happier, and do better in school?"

2. Complete the Physical strategy Warning Signs (p. 25) as a group. Ask each child to complete his or her own individual worksheet.

3. Process the experience and share warning signs together when finished. Discuss how this strategy can be used in real-life situations.

4. Assign homework: At the next session, each group member will be asked to give two examples of situations where they were able to recognize their warning signs. Ask them to write the examples and the warning signs down and share them at the beginning of the next session.

Session 2

1. Quickly review the homework assignment from Session 1.

2. Continue to focus on the Physical skills and complete the Melting Freeze strategy (p. 23) together.

3. Discuss how this strategy can be implemented when we recognize that our warning signs are starting.

4. Assign homework: Practice Melting Freeze two times before the next session.

The focus for the next two sessions is on feelings identification and the idea that we have control over how we choose to express our emotions.

Session 3

1. Quickly review the homework assignment from the last session.

2. Let the group know that this week's focus is on feelings.

3. Complete the Emotional strategy You Can't Make Me Laugh (p. 37) together. Be sure that each child becomes aware that they control their own feelings.

4. Complete the Emotional strategy Feelings Clip Art (p. 40) together. This strategy helps children identify and label emotions accurately.

5. Assign homework: Identify an example of a situation where they exercised control over an emotion. Remind them to label the emotion accurately.

Session 4

1. Quickly review the homework assignment from the last session.

2. Complete the Emotional strategy Free Healthy Expression (p. 55).

3. Summarize this Emotional section by discussing how we do have control of our feelings and how important it is to identify and express them in healthy ways.

4. Assign homework: Write down an example of expressing an emotion in a healthy way.

The focus for the next two sessions is on the development of Cognitive skills. Keep in mind that not all children progress to this level of self-regulation. To prevent frustration and failure, know what your group is capable of. If they are not ready, continue to solidify their skills within the Physical and Emotional Domains.

Session 5

1. Quickly review the homework assignment from the last session. Let them know that this week the strategies will be about thinking, planning and problem-solving.

2. Complete the Cognitive strategy Finish Your Thoughts (p. 63). This should help begin to show them how our thoughts guide our feelings and behaviors.

3. Discuss how we can change our feelings by changing our thoughts.

4. Assign homework: Practice the strategy Melting Freeze.

Session 6

1. Quickly review the homework assignment from the last session.

2. Choose one of the other Cognitive Strategies that seems to be relevant to the group of children you are working with. For example, if they tend to feed off of each other and get into trouble, you may want to do Don't Take the Bait (p. 57).

3. Process the outcome and main idea of the strategy you chose. If time allows, you can do more than one.

4. Assign homework: Teach the strategy Melting Freeze to another person.

> The final two sessions are designed to help the group put all of the self-regulation skills together.

Session 7

1. Quickly review the homework assignment from the last session.

2. Role-play two of the following events and process them together using the Event Processing Worksheet (p. 105) as a guide:

   a. A child is not picked for a team to play in a game at recess
   b. One child makes fun of another child for saying the wrong answer
   c. A child drops all of his/her books in front of the class
   d. A child is asked to speak in front of the whole class for the first time
   e. A child sees his/her parents arguing very loudly

3. Also role-play through each of the self-regulation strategies the group is able to identify. Monitor how the group progresses through each section. This will give you valuable information about who may need more help and what concepts may need to be reinforced.

4. Assign homework: Let someone else know how you express Anger in a healthy way. Identify a situation from your life that has happened recently for the group to discuss next time.

Session 8

1. Review the homework assignment.

2. Role-play as many of the "real-life" examples that the group members have brought to the session as part of the homework assignment. Also role-play through the strategies they would use.

3. Draw specific attention to the Physical, Emotional, and Cognitive strategies the group decides to implement to cope with the situation. Take notes for the group during the process on a whiteboard, or another place where everyone can see the process. Use the Event Processing Worksheet (p. 105) as a guide.

4. Process the progress the group has made over the past few weeks. Celebrate the successes.

5. Handout the Self-regulator Certificates (p. 107) to the individuals in the group. Celebrate the effort and challenge them to continue to develop the skills they have learned.

6. If possible, continue to follow up with the group members over the next few weeks.

Appendix A

Problem/Strategy Matrix

	Strategies	Anger & Aggression	Anxiety & Worry	Self-esteem & Sadness	Social Interaction & Bullying	Oppositional & Impulse Control	Page no.
P H Y S I C A L	Cooling the Flame	S	R		R	S	19
	Melting Freeze	S	S		R	S	23
	Warning Signs	S	S	S	R	S	25
	Take a Hike	S	S	R	S	S	28
	A Safe Place	R	S	R	S		31
	Animal Stretches	S	S			R	34
E M O T I O N A L	You Can't Make Me Laugh	S		S	S	R	37
	Feelings Clip Art	S	S	S			40
	The Emotional Safe	S	S	S			43
	Emotional Rain Gauge	S	S	R			46
	Emotional Knots	S	S	S	S	R	49
	Emotional Overflow	S	R		R	R	51
	Free Emotional Expression	S	S	S	S	S	53
C O G N I T I V E	Don't Take the Bait	S		R	S	S	57
	Defiance Trap	S				S	60
	Finish Your Thoughts	S	S	S			63
	The Domino Effect	S	S	S	S	S	68
	Magnetic Thoughts	R	S	S		R	71
	Detection Radar	R	S		S		74
	Shaping Your Thoughts	R	S	S			76
	Problem Solving Remote	R	R	R	S	S	81
	Grow a Thought		S	S	R		84
	Target Practice	S	S	S	R		87

S = Specifically designed to target problem area

R = Related and useful for problem area

Appendix B

Assessment/Progress Monitoring Tool

Rate each on a scale of 1 to 10 with 10 being well-developed.

	Behaviors To Address	1st Rating (1-10)	Strategy Used (See Matrix)	Response	Outcome Rating (1-10)
PHYSICAL					
Recognizes physical signs					
Uses healthy calming strategies successfully					
EMOTIONAL					
Identifies feelings					
Recognizes responsibility and ability to change					
Expresses Emotions in healthy ways					
COGNITIVE					
Replaces Unhealthy thoughts with healthy beliefs					
Uses Cognitive strategies to problem-solve					
STRENGTHS:			**BARRIERS:**		

Appendix C

Diagram of Self-regulation Training Philosophy

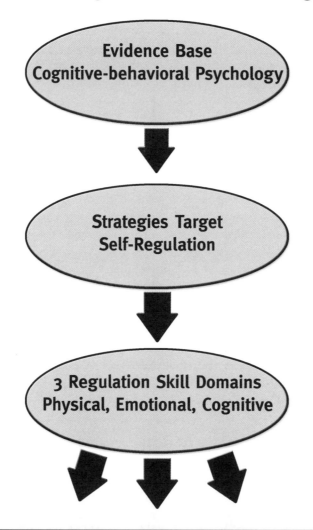

Evidence Base
Cognitive-behavioral Psychology

↓

Strategies Target
Self-Regulation

↓

3 Regulation Skill Domains
Physical, Emotional, Cognitive

Academic Performance	Emotional Control	Motivation
Aggression/Violence	Executive Function	School Safety
Anger	Impulse Control	Self-efficacy
Anxiety	Learned Helplessness	Self-esteem
Attention	Locus of Control	Social interaction
Attribution	Longevity	Success
Cognitive Flexibility	Happiness	Trauma
Depression	Oppositional Defiance	Well-being

Appendix D

Parent Letter

Dear Parent or Guardian:

This letter is to inform you that your child has been given the opportunity to participate in an interactive Self-regulation Training Program. This program utilizes interactive, engaging activities to increase your child's ability to:

- Physically calm down when he/she is upset
- Identify and express his/her emotions appropriately
- Implement problem-solving skills and gain understanding

The program consists of 8 brief sessions (15-30 minutes each).

Program Summary:

Week 1 – Develop physical calming skills
Week 2 – Learn to accurately identify feelings and express them in healthy ways
Week 3 – Learn problem-solving skills specific to problem areas
Week 4 – Practice and reinforce Self-regulation skills

Research indicates that those with well-developed Self-regulation skills:

- Have better academic performance
- Do better socially
- Have fewer mental health issues
- Live longer, happier lives

As with all things involving children, parental involvement is the key to success. Your child will be asked to speak with you about what he/she is learning. We would like to thank you for taking part in this important step toward preparing your child with the tools to cope with the challenges that he/she will face in life.

Sincerely,

Appendix E

Self-regulation Training Contract for Change

I _____, agree that over the next few weeks I will try my best to help myself by learning these important skills. When I complete my training I will be able to calm myself down, express my feelings in healthy ways, and create solutions for some of the things I've been struggling with.

Together, use the next few lines to briefly describe a situation that has been troubling you. It could be something that you would like to learn how to solve on your own.

_____

_____

COMPLETE THE LOWER PORTION AFTER YOU HAVE COMPLETED YOUR TRAINING.

Describe a recent situation to process:

1. What happened?

_____

_____

2. How did your body feel?

_____

3. What were your feelings? And how much? Feelings: _____ _____ _____
   How much (1-10)? _____

4. What were your thoughts about what happened?

_____

Self-regulation Strategies:

1. Physical – What did you do to calm your body down? How did you do?

_____

_____

2. Emotions – What did you do to express your feelings? Was it healthy?

_____

_____

3. Cognitive – Were your thoughts about the event accurate and healthy? What's the plan if this happens again?

_____

_____

Appendix F

Event Processing Worksheet

Information:

1. What happened?

_____

_____

2. Any Warning Signs?

_____

3. What did you feel? And how much? Feelings: _____ _____ _____

   How much (1-10)? _____

4. What were your thoughts about what happened?

_____

_____

Self-regulation Strategies:

1. Physical – What did you do to calm your body down? How did you do?

_____

_____

2. Emotions – What did you do to express your feelings? Was it healthy?

_____

_____

3. Cognitive – Were your thoughts about the event accurate and healthy? What's the plan if this happens again?

_____

_____

Appendix G

My Self-regulation Strategies

Physical – These are the things I can do to calm my body down:

1. _____

2. _____

3. _____

Emotions – These are the things that help me figure out my feelings and express them in healthy ways:

1. _____

2. _____

3. _____

Cognitive Skills – These are things that help me figure out the answers to problems, or things I need to remember about myself:

1. _____

2. _____

3. _____

Appendix H

Congratulations to

_____

*for successfully
completing the Self-regulation
Training Program on*

_____

(date)

*You now have the skills you need to control
your body, your feelings, and your thoughts.*

REMEMBER THAT SELF-REGULATION=SUCCESS!

Self-regulation = Success

3 STEPS

1. Body
2. Feelings
3. Thoughts

References

Bailey, B. A., (2001). *Conscious discipline: 7 basic skills for brain smart classroom management.* Oviedo, Fl: Loving Guidance, Inc.

Baumeister, R. F., Heatherton, T. F., & Tice, D. M. (1994). *Losing control: How and why people fail at self-regulation.* San Diego: Academic Press.

Beck, R., & Fernandez, E. (1998). Cognitive-behavioral therapy in the treatment of anger: A meta-analysis. *Cognitive Therapy and Research*, 22(1), 63-74.

Butler, A. C., Chapman, J. E., Forman, E. M., & Beck, A. T. (2006). The empirical status of cognitive-behavioral therapy: A review of meta-analysis. *Clinical Psychology Review*, 26, 17-31.

Cannon, W. B. (1932). *The Wisdom of the Body.* New York: W.W. Norton.

Duckworth, A. L. & Seligman, M. E. (2005). Self-discipline outdoes IQ in predicting academic performance in adolescents. *Psychological Science*, 16(12), 939-944.

Ellis, A. (1962). *Reason and emotion in psychotherapy.* Secaucus, NJ: Citadel Press, Pages 24-32.

Goleman, D. (1998). *Working with emotional intelligence.* New York: Bantam Books.

Greene, R. W., & Ablon, J. S. (2006). *Treating explosive kids: The collaborative problem solving approach.* New York: The Gilford Press.

Grossarth-Maticek, R. & Eysenck, H. J. (1995). Self-regulation and mortality from cancer, coronary heart disease, and other causes: *A prospective study. Personality and Individual Differences*, 19(6), 781-795.

Hubble, M.A., Duncan, B.L., & Miller, S.D. (eds.) (1999). *The heart and soul of change: What works in therapy.* Washington, D.C.: APA Press.

Kuhl, J. (1984). Volitional aspects of achievement motivation and learned helplessness: Toward a comprehensive theory of action control. In B. A. Maher (Ed.), *Progress in experimental personality research* (Vol. 13, pp. 99-171). New York, NY: Academic Press.

Macklem, G. L. (2008). *Practitioner's guide to emotion regulation in school-aged children.* New York, NY: Springer.

Masten, A. S., & Coatsworth, J. D. (1998). The development of competence in favorable and unfavorable environments: Lessons from research on successful children. *American Psychologist*, 53, 205-220.

Moffitt, T. E., Arseneault, L., Belsky, D., Dickson, N., Hancox, R. J., Harrington, H., Poulton, R., Roberts, B. W., Ross, S., Sears, M. R., Thomson, W. M., & Caspi, A. (2011, February). A gradient of childhood self-control predicts health, wealth, and public safety. *Proceedings of the National Academy of Sciences*, 108(7), 2693-2698.

Perry, B. D. (2006). The neurosequential model of therapeutics: Applying principles of neurodevelopment to clinical work with maltreated and traumatized children. In N. B. Webb (Ed.), *Working with traumatized youth in child welfare* (pp. 27-52). New York, NY: The Guilford Press.

Shonkoff, J. P., Phillips, D., & National Research Council (U.S.). (2000). *From neurons to neighborhoods: The science of early child development.* Washington, D.C: National Academy Press.

Yerkes, R.M. & Dodson, J.D. (1908). The relation of strength of stimulus to rapidity of habit-formation. *Journal of Comparative Neurology and Psychology*, 18, 459-482.

About the Authors

Brad Chapin, M.S. is a husband and a father of three. He is a Masters Level Psychologist and Licensed Clinical Psychotherapist. He is an author, a speaker and also the creator of the Challenge Software Program for children. This interactive, web-based tool utilizes animated scenarios and games to engage children quickly and teach them the fundamentals of self-regulation. The program is referenced in the book and continues to evolve. It can be found at www.cpschallenge.com.

Brad has been working with individuals and families for over 10 years. He spends a great deal of time training school counselors, teachers, mental health professionals and parents how to implement self-regulation strategies successfully. He also serves as the Director for Community-based Services for his local Community Mental Health Center where he oversees children's mental health services delivered by 75 staff members in the homes, schools, and communities throughout a five-county area.

Email: brad.chapin@cpschallenge.com

Matthew L. Penner, M.S.W. is husband and father of two. He is a Licensed Master Social Worker, providing services in community mental health center focusing on child, adolescent, and family therapy interventions. He specializes in childhood onset disorders including ADHD, anxiety, mood, and behavioral disorders. Further, he has professional experience in residential treatment centers, therapeutic group homes, medical facilities, and community mental health. Additionally, Matthew has spent time training other professionals in the areas of crisis intervention and cultural diversity.